THE COMPLETE BOOK OF
MUSTANG

BEEKMAN HOUSE

Louis Weber, C.E.O.
Publications International, Ltd.
7373 North Cicero Avenue
Lincolnwood, Illinois 60646

Permission is never granted for commercial purposes.

Manufactured in Yugoslavia.

h   g   f   e   d   c   b   a

ISBN 0-517-67668-0

This edition published by Beekman House,
Distributed by Crown Publishers,Inc.,
225 Park Avenue South, New York,
New York 10003

Library of Congress Catalog Card Number:
88-63580

CREDITS

Photography

The editors gratefully acknowledge Thomas Glatch, Bud Juneau, Milton Gene Kieft, Vince Manocchi, Doug Mitchel, Dick Nesbitt, Joseph H. Wherry, and Nicky Wright. Special thanks to Ford Motor Company, Public Relations Department; Chuck Ordowski, Ford Photomedia; and Dave Schmerler, Schmerler Ford, Elk Grove Village, Illinois.

Owners

Special thanks to the owners of the cars featured in this book for their enthusiastic cooperation: Doug & Teresa Avidston, Duane Baker, Ken Baker, Michael Baker, John & Kathy Baltes, Dennis Begley, Don Bergman, D. L. Bohart, Rex Bolan, Jim Buhle, Dean & Wandy Casey, Ron Chamerlik, Charles & Marie Cobb, Bill Collins, Ed Coughlin, Chris Dawalt, Ron Edgerly, Gary Emerson, Richard A. Emry, Clarence E. Ferguson, Ray P. Fisher, Alice Greunke, Tom Haase, Kurt A. Havely, Greg & Rhonda Haynes, Biff & Donna Hitzeman, Bob Hoffman, Winfred & Betty Keul, Gerald King, Donald Kish Sr., Leroy Lasiter, George Lyons, Duanne Mann, Darl & Mary McAllister, Ronald E. Miller, Tina Miller, Rick Mitchell, Alan Nelson, Don Nixon, Gary Pahee, Jay F. Painter, Gary Pattee, Robert & Julie Peters, Thomas E. & Carol A. Podemski, Dixen Polderman, Bob Porter, Thomas S. Rapala, Dennis Roxworthy, Thomas S. Rupala, Jason Saunder, Jim & Ginger Schoenherr, Stephen Schonegg, Robert L. Schutt, James P. Scott, Wendy Talarico, Frank Trummer, Greg Turley, Larry Wilson, Ron Wold, and Mark Wyatt.

CONTENTS

INTRODUCTION 6

CHAPTER ONE
Before the Mustang:
Distant Hoofbeats 10

CHAPTER TWO
Designing a Legend:
False Starts, a Fabulous Finish 34

CHAPTER THREE
1965-66:
Hi Yo, Ponycar! 56

CHAPTER FOUR
1967-68:
More and Less 88

CHAPTER FIVE
1969-70:
Horses for Courses 110

CHAPTER SIX
1971-73:
From Quarter Horse to Clydesdale 142

CHAPTER SEVEN
1974-78:
Back to the Future 166

CHAPTER EIGHT
1979-81:
A Legend Reborn 196

CHAPTER NINE
1982-86:
The Boss Returns 230

CHAPTER TEN
1987-89:
Galloping into the Future 260

CHAPTER ELEVEN
The Shelby-Mustangs
1965-70: Short-Lived Thoroughbreds . . . 280

INDEX 316

The Boss 302 became the Boss 351 for '71. Unfortunately, Ford pulled out of racing, so this would be the last Boss.

INTRODUCTION

This book appears in the Mustang's 25th anniversary year, 1989. For us older "baby boomers" especially, it's sobering to realize that that much time has passed since Ford began a legend with the first "ponycar" (a term coined, incidentally, by *Car Life* magazine). Seems like it was only yesterday.

Ford was definitely up to something in the spring of 1964, that much we knew. Enthusiast magazines had been showing us a parade of tantalizing Ford experiments for over two years—"not for production" show cars that were still somehow too complete, too detailed, too *finished* to be anything other than a prelude to a new showroom model.

But what might that be? A two-seat MG-style roadster, like the mid-engine Mustang I? A smaller T-Bird, like the Allegro X-car? A sleek fastback to challenge the Corvette Sting Ray, like the Cobra II? Perhaps a sporty 2+2 convertible like the Mustang II shown the previous fall at Watkins Glen.

Then, suddenly, there it was in *Time* magazine, of all places: a neat-looking black convertible in a hazy "spy" photo. It only showed the rear, alas, but the story said that this was the new sporty Ford that was going to sell for little more than a pedestrian economy compact. It seemed to good to be true.

Yet amazingly, it *was* true, and within days we got a look at the whole car in a splashy two-page color ad. "Presenting the unexpected," it read. "New Ford Mustang! $2368 f.o.b Detroit." Wow! Sporty good looks, six-cylinder economy, available V-8 go, lots of nifty standard features and more luxury and performance extras than you could shake a checkbook at—all at a price most anyone could afford. Even the muscular steed galloping along the grille, front fenders, and on the exposed tail-mount gas cap seemed right. "Mustang has the look, the fire, the flavor of the great European road cars," read that announcement ad. "Yet it's as American as its name...and as practical as its price." Seldom has advertising been so truthful.

To those not yet born in early 1964, or those too young to have developed much awareness of cars, the enormous impact of that first Mustang may be hard to appreciate. But enormous it was. Quite simply, everybody, overnight, went *crazy* for Ford's new sporty one, and it wasn't long before you started seeing them on the road (in fact, almost from the day after the April 17 public unveiling at the New York World's Fair). College guys drove 'em. College girls, too. But then, this was a "young person's" car. The real surprise was the number of working women, middle-age businessmen, even senior citizens who bought Mustangs.

Dealers couldn't write orders fast enough, and Dearborn worked overtime as buyers rushed to be the first in their crowd to put a Mustang in the driveway. Not since 1949 had a Ford so thoroughly excited so many people. Suddenly it seemed a whole nation had a little extra spring in its step. And we needed that; with the tragedy of November 22, 1963, still so horribly vivid in our collective consciousness, the Mustang was a welcome escape.

And immensely popular, of course: over a million sold for that first extra-long model year (April 1964-August 1965)—a new industry record. Small wonder. As that ad so succinctly put it, "The basic Mustang is an eminently practical and economical car, yet it was designed to be designed by you. You can make your Mustang into a luxury or high-performance car by selecting from a large but reasonably priced group of options." It was a masterstroke for the age of "do your own thing," the key to the whole Mustang concept and a big reason for the car's astounding initial success.

As for the ever-jaded "buff books" that had run all those preview stories, they generally liked the finished product, too. A few groused about the humble underpinnings borrowed from the compact Falcon, but they were as captivated as the

The Mustang, here a '65, thundered on to the American auto market with such gusto that it sired a whole new breed, the ponycar. Now 25 years old, it's still galloping at a torrid pace.

public by Mustang's lithe lines, "personal" character and affordable versatility. "Easily the best thing to come out of Dearborn since the 1932 V-8 Model B roadster," gushed *Car and Driver*. Said the stringback-driving-gloves-and-tweedy-cap set at *Road & Track*: "The Mustang is definitely a sports car, on par in most respects with such undisputed types as the MG-B, Triumph TR-4 or Sunbeam Alpine."

Car Life probably summed it up best: "In concept, the Mustang draws from the original Thunderbird and the [recent Chevrolet] Corvair Monza; in execution, it has ancestry in the [Ford] Fairlane and Lincoln Continental; and in appearance, it reflects the Continental Mark II...A market that has been looking for a car has it now...[Mustang] may well be, in fact, better than any domestically mass-produced automobile on the basis of handling and roadability and performance per dollar invested."

But trend-setters are never long without imitators, and this plus Detroit's usual "bigger-is-better" urges inevitably produced a big change in Mustang's character—literally. By 1969, the original ponycar had become another muscle car; with the even larger new 1971 design, it was in danger of becoming another Thunderbird. Yet much of this quarter-horse-to-Clydesdale metamorphosis was only dictated by market tastes and Ford's own research. And it wasn't all bad. The jazzy Mach 1 and race-inspired Boss 302 were among the hottest and most exciting cars of their day. Ditto the limited-production GT-350s and GT-500s, very special Mustangs as individual as the former race-car driver who built them, an iconoclastic Texan named Carroll Shelby.

Nevertheless, the world was changing fast by the early Seventies, and Mustang seemed to be changing in the wrong directions—fatter and thirstier when thin was starting to be "in" and thrifty nifty. This pattern did not go unnoticed by the public, the press, even Ford stockholders. The story is told of how one of the last, a '65 Mustang owner named Anna Muccioli, got up before Henry Ford II at the company's 1968 annual meeting and pointedly asked, "Why can't you just leave a sports car small? I mean you keep blowing them up and starting another little one, blow that one up and start another one. I mean,

why don't you just *leave* them?" Her remarks drew cheers—and this stammering reply from the chairman: "We will keep in mind what you say here and, hopefully, we will have a product that will be satisfactory to you."

It took a few years, but Ford would: the new-for-'74 Mustang II. But though more like the original than any Mustang since 1968, it didn't have the same magic, didn't fire the public's imagination as much, wasn't anywhere near a national sensation. Blame the styling if you must (as many have)—a lumpy small-scale caricature of '65. Blame reduced performance, the dulled spirit of those times, the many sporty import coupes lately on the scene. Even so,

the Mustang II sold consistently and well—sometimes *very* well—over a five-year run. Arriving as it did almost on the eve of the world's first great energy crisis, it was timely to say the least. And with the first four-cylinder engine in Mustang history, it seemed to forecast the future.

Mustang's ultimate future—at least as we know it so far—arrived for 1979 in an all-new fifth-generation design (minus the Roman numeral). It was a little larger and more restrained than the II. Demonstrably sleeker as well, thanks to Ford's growing interest in the growing science of auto aerodynamics. It was, in fact, something you'd expect more from Ford Europe than Ford Dearborn, yet still very much in the

tradition of the inaugural '65: sporty, tight, practical, versatile, interesting, affordable.

Like the II, this Mustang bowed just months before a fuel panic (call it "Energy Crisis II") and sales suffered for a few years after 1979. Performance suffered too, another symptom of Detroit's malaise in that period. But for 1982, Ford looked to its own history and began pushing "Total Performance" again, with Mustang leading the way, of course. The result: A company that had been down on its financial knees made an impressive comeback that continues even at this writing. Mustang also bounced back, not only in performance and pizzazz but sales. By 1986 it was roundly outselling the latest versions of

the only other Sixties ponycars to survive the Seventies, the Chevrolet Camaro and Pontiac Firebird—and they were newer designs. No doubt about it: The magic was back. Mustang had come full circle.

These are only the highlights of the Mustang story that unfolds in the following pages. Our thanks to the Ford Motor Company Design Center and Photomedia Department for supplying the many historical photographs shown. Our thanks also to the owners of the restored Mustangs pictured throughout for making their cars available to us for photography.

In an age where too many things come and go all too quickly, it's somewhat comforting to observe that the Mustang in

its 25th year is again very much the sort of car we loved in its first year. Even more heartening, it seems destined to be around for a good many years *more*. We should all be so lucky.

The Auto Editors of CONSUMER GUIDE®
January 1989

The Mustang will survive pretty much as is (*above*) into the early '90s. Ford made a major commitment to upgrade its Dearborn assembly plant, a sure sign that there is a Mustang in Ford's future. Likely, it will be restyled on a shortened Thunderbird platform around 1991 and that it will get Ford's upcoming "modular" V-8.

CHAPTER ONE

Before
the Mustang:
Distant Hoofbeats

There's more to the Mustang story than a casual observer may believe. Indeed, the original ponycar did not begin with the experimental Mustang I of 1962, nor with the two-seat Thunderbird of 1955-57, though both have a place in the Mustang story. The tale actually begins with developments as early as 1946, when the American auto industry emerged from World War II into an age of unbridled optimism.

When the nation returned to civilian production in late 1945, all-new models just didn't make sense for most automakers. Prewar body dies were still available—and little used in many cases, which made it uneconomical to scrap them. And though most companies had managed to steal time from their war work to evolve new designs from their stillborn plans for 1943-45, none were needed right away. After four long years of doing without, the public was simply starved for new cars (and other consumer goods), resulting in an unprecedented seller's market that eagerly gobbled up most anything on wheels. This explains why Detroit merely fielded warmed-over '42s for the first postwar model year, 1946. Only Studebaker among

prewar makes issued a complete redesign early, for 1947.

Once the huge, pent-up demand began to be satisfied though, the seller's market waned and buyers started hungering for new engineering and new styling. Indeed, Detroit and the popular press had teased the public with wartime promises of a bright, prosperous, technologically wondrous postwar world filled with futuristic cars that would appear right after hostilities ended. Still, it wasn't until 1949 that the Big Three—Ford, Chrysler, and General Motors—offered entirely new models.

In getting back to peacetime business, some automakers considered how their prewar designs could be made to appear new, at least on the surface. The result was a spate of limited-production specials, standard models made more glamorous via a few relatively simple styling changes, created to maintain buyer interest in an otherwise familiar group of cars. Chrysler, Ford, and Nash each fielded one for 1946. All had conventional production bodies modified with structural wood, built much like the woody wagons of the day. This invariably comprised a framework of white ash, maple, or yellow birch and inserts of

real mahogany wood or woodgrain decals.

Nash's Suburban and Chrysler's Town & Country were sedans on wheelbases about 10 feet long and powered by middle-sized L-head sixes. Chrysler also offered a Town & Country convertible on an even longer chassis with a big straight eight. Chrysler sold over 12,000 Town & Countrys through 1948, while Nash moved a mere 1000 Suburbans. Despite their modest volume, these cars served their intended purpose of stimulating showroom traffic until their makers' first all-postwar models arrived for 1949. Though Nash dropped the Suburban that year, Chrysler continued the T&C convertible and added a hardtop version for 1950, after which it abandoned woodies of all kinds and applied Town & Country to all-steel station wagons.

After World War II, automakers could sell anything on four wheels. Still, they tried to make the worked-over '42s look fresh. The woody look was one way, as seen on the '46 Nash Suburban (*below*), the 1947-48 Ford Sportsman (*opposite, bottom*), and the 1950 Chrysler Town & Country (*top*).

13

The first postwar limited editions from the makers of the future Mustang were the Ford and Mercury Sportsman convertibles. These were inspired by a customized Model A built during the war by then-styling director Bob Gregorie. Henry Ford II, just released from the Navy to help salvage the ailing Ford Motor Company, was searching for something to spice up his staid, carryover postwar model lines. After seeing Gregorie's wood-trimmed custom, he ordered a similar treatment for production and the Sportsman was born. The planking was no problem, as Ford owned a forest in Northern Michigan that had supplied the raw material for its wagon bodies since 1929.

Offered only for 1946, the Mercury Sportsman saw but 205 copies. It rode a longer wheelbase and was heavier than Ford's version but used the same 100-horsepower flathead V-8, so it didn't perform as well. It was also priced more than $200 higher, which may explain why it didn't significantly contribute to Mercury sales traffic.

Ford's Sportsman, on the other hand, was a minor success, with close to 3500 built for 1946-48. Again, such volume wasn't as significant as the much-needed touch of glamour it brought to neighborhood showrooms. The Sportsman was phased out in early 1948 in preparation

for Ford's all-new '49 line, which didn't need a special for sales zest, though a closed continuation, perhaps with simulated wood trim, was briefly contemplated.

Yet the very next year, Dearborn was back with a pack of limited editions: the Ford Custom Crestliner, Mercury Monterey, and the Lincoln Lido and Capri. Each was essentially a customized rendition of the standard two-door sedan. The Crestliner sported a bold two-tone color scheme, with a contrasting bodyside sweep and a padded, color-keyed vinyl top. Monterey and the Lincolns offered a choice of padded tops in canvas or leather, plus more deluxe interiors. All contrived to provide the appearance and sporty feel of a true convertible in lieu of a pillarless "hardtop convertible," the innovative body style introduced at GM during 1949 and already selling at a rapid clip.

Responding more directly to that initia-

Opposite page: By 1950, the hardtop craze was underway. Ford didn't have one, so it dressed up a two-door sedan with bright two-toning, vinyl roof, and a deluxe interior —and called it the Crestliner (*top*). Lincoln, using the same approach, brought out the Lido, here a '51 (*bottom*). Lincoln finally got a hardtop for '52, here a top-line Capri (*above*). Mercury's sportiest '53 was the Monterey ragtop (*below*).

tive, Ford introduced its own hardtop for 1951, the Victoria. However, it retained all the padded-top specials that year, though none were successful and all would be dropped after '51. Mercury and Lincoln got hardtops with their 1952 redesign, when the Monterey and Capri designations became series names. The Crestliner bowed out after 1951 volume of just 8703 units (versus 17,601 for 1950).

Aside from Nash's Suburban, the independents offered no noteworthy limited editions before 1949, when newcomer Kaiser-Frazer, which began production in 1946 at Willow Run, Michigan, weighed in with the Kaiser Virginian. This stemmed from management's prior decision to make a convertible sedan out of K-F's pillared, fixed-roof four-door, but its engineering was of the patchwork variety, as shown by the need for a ponderous, reinforced frame to prevent body flex. As a spinoff from the convertible, the Virginian was the first four-

door "hardtop sedan," though both models had small, fixed, metal-framed glass B-pillars. Like the Crestliner, this so-called hardtop offered an optional roof cover simulating a convertible top, and most were so equipped. But at $3000, the Virginian was prohibitively expensive for

its day, and only 1000 were sold through 1950.

The "personal" Kaiser for 1951 was the Dragon, initially a trim package for the upper-series Deluxe four-door sedan and distinguished from other models only by its interior. Seats, door panels, and

Opposite page: Specialty models were common in the early Fifties. Ford's response to Chevy's Bel Air hardtop was the fast-selling Victoria (*top*). Kaiser-Frazer debuted the first four-door hardtop (with fixed-glass center post), here a '49 Kaiser Virginian (*bottom*). *This page:* Another specialty model from Kaiser was the '53 Dragon (*top*). The '53 Packard Caribbean (*bottom*) would be called a personal-luxury car today.

dashboard were covered with embossed "dragon" vinyl, the name chosen to avoid confusion with the skin of alligators, whose survival was of concern even then. As the first car from a major Detroit producer to use vinyl as an upholstery material, it started a trend that would quickly spread throughout the industry.

Later that season, K-F offered a "Mark II" Dragon sporting a vinyl top as well as a vinyl interior. The pattern was now called "dinosaur," so there would be no mistaking it for the hide of any endangered species. A later version with bamboo-like trim was called the Jade Dragon. Though all these cars were slow sellers, they at least kept customers coming in.

Kaiser skipped a limited edition for 1952, then revived the series with the "Hardtop Dragon." Taking a cue from Ford, K-F promoted this four-door sedan

17

as a hardtop by virtue of its padded "bambu" vinyl top. Richly upholstered, the '53 Dragon was gilded with gold-plated medallions and hood ornament, and carried a gold owner's nameplate on its dash. But at some $3800, it fared about as poorly as the Virginian. Fewer than 1300 were built, and many were left unsold at the end of the model year.

But 1953 saw a raft of limited-edition "personal" cars from other makers. Packard, for example, bowed its svelte Caribbean, a convertible that took many of its styling themes from the interesting Pan American two-seater, which had been

developed with the Henney Body Company in 1952 for publicity purposes under the hard-driving leadership of Packard's new president James J. Nance. Listing at $5200 and equipped with a potent 180-bhp straight eight, the Caribbean stood apart from standard Packard convertibles with its elegant trim, ultra-clean lines and a custom hood with full-width air scoop. A star attraction at Packard showrooms, the Caribbean continued for 1954 with an even larger 212-bhp engine. Production was low—just 750 of the '53s and only 400 of the '54s—but it was an important prestige offering, helping convince all and

sundry that Packard was serious about regaining its preeminence in the luxury market.

The Caribbean was restyled for 1955 and, like the rest of that year's Packard line, benefited from the firm's first-ever overhead-valve V-8 with 275 bhp. For 1956, power rose to 310. Convertible prices remained at around $6000, and a companion Caribbean hardtop arrived at about $5500. But falling sales of the higher-volume models and tight finances resulting from Packard's purchase of Studebaker in 1954 condemned the Caribbean to extinction after '56.

General Motors was certainly the personal car's strongest exponent in the early Fifties, four of its five divisions offering limited-production specials in 1953 alone: Cadillac Eldorado, Buick Skylark, Oldsmobile Fiesta, and Chevrolet Corvette. All were mainly intended to test public reaction to certain styling and engineering ideas intended for near-term mass-market models.

Boasting a custom leather interior and a tuned, 170-bhp version of Oldsmobile's famed Rocket V-8, the $5700 Fiesta was one of the first production cars with a wraparound windshield. Also included as standard were Hydra-Matic transmission

General Motors fielded three specialty convertibles in 1953. The Cadillac Eldorado (*bottom left*) was largely custom built, sported a wraparound windshield, and sold for a towering $7750, $3606 more than the Series Sixty-Two ragtop. Buick's entry was the $5000 Skylark (*bottom right*). Cadillac sold 532 units, Buick moved 1690. Packard's posh '55 Patrician (*opposite, top*) sold for $5932; 500 were built.

and power brakes, steering, windows, and seats. But the Fiesta was cancelled after only one year and a mere 458 units. Division managers had apparently decided they didn't need a limited edition to reach the typical Olds buyer, who was thought to be somewhat less interested in personal expression than Buick or Cadillac prospects.

The Skylark was more ambitious: basically the standard Roadmaster convertible with circular rear wheel openings and Kelsey-Hayes wire wheels (also used on Packard's Caribbean), plus a cut-down windshield (not wrapped, though), the finest quality upholstery, and four fewer inches in overall length. Only 1690 of the '53s were built, priced at $5000 a copy. It

returned in Buick's rebodied '54 line on the shorter Special/Century chassis, with new square-rigged styling, wrapped front glass and a lot more glitz than the '53, but without most of its exclusive touches, though the last allowed Buick to trim the price to $4500. But even that didn't boost demand, and the Skylark was cancelled at mid-season after only 836 sales, a standard Century convertible taking its place.

Cadillac's Eldorado was by far the most successful of GM's 1953 personal-car quartet and, as such, would strongly influence product planners at Ford. Conceived as an upper-crust specialty item, it arrived at an astronomical $7750, which helps explain why only 432 were sold that first year. Like Fiesta and Skylark, it used

the standard convertible body with a cut-down, wraparound windshield, but was unique in having a metal cover that concealed the stowed top, imparting a smoother look to the rear deck.

Taking advantage of the '53's prestige, Cadillac decided to make the Eldorado more salable for '54. Like that year's Skylark, it was more like the standard issue, but sales improved thanks to a retail price trimmed by no less than $2000. Exactly 2000 of the '54s were sold, followed by 4000 of the '55s and 6000 for '56 (the last bolstered by the addition of a Seville hardtop coupe; that year's convertible was retitled Eldorado Biarritz).

After '54, Eldorados were easily distinguished from other Cadillacs by a distinc-

tive rear end with sharply pointed fins, plus a slightly more powerful version of the division's brawny V-8. For 1957-58, Cadillac fielded the even more upmarket Eldorado Brougham, a close-coupled hardtop sedan selling for $13,000, but at that price only 704 were called for (plus another 200 of the restyled 1959-60 version, built by Pinin Farina in Italy). Both the Brougham and Seville vanished after 1960, yet Eldorado sales rose to significant levels. For 1967 came a new front-wheel-drive Eldorado. Based on Oldsmobile's pioneering Toronado platform, it became one of the most successful high-priced personal cars in history. Not surprisingly, it's with us still.

Besides big, flashy convertibles and

hardtops, the sports car had also captured the public's fancy by the mid-Fifties. The popularity of the MGs and Jaguars brought home from England by returning GIs prompted other European sports models aimed squarely at American buyers, notably the Triumph TR2, Austin-Healey 100,

Sports cars began to capture America's fancy in the Fifties. Chevrolet responded in 1953 with the six-cylinder, fiberglass-bodied Corvette (*opposite*). Among the foreign contenders were (*this page, top left and clockwise*) the sleek Jaguar XK-120, the affordable MGA, the gutsy Triumph TR2, and the powerful Austin-Healey.

Alfa Romeo Giulietta, and Mercedes-Benz 190SL. Although sports cars accounted for only .027 percent of the U.S. market in 1953, there was a growing fascination with "foreign" features like bucket seats, floor-mounted gearshifts, and lithe two-seat bodies on chassis with handling verve virtually unknown on this side of the Atlantic. Detroit's marketing mavens began to wonder whether sporty cars might help sales even more than customized specials.

Sports cars were quick to appear from two independents: the Anglo-American Nash-Healey of 1951 and the fiberglass-bodied, sliding-door Kaiser-Darrin of 1954. A somewhat different attempt was the very low-volume Hudson Italia of 1954-55, a four-seat grand touring coupe with jazzy, rectilinear American styling executed by Italy's Carrozzeria Touring on the compact Hudson Jet chassis. We should also not forget 1953's new low-slung Starlight coupe and Starliner hardtop from the Raymond Loewy studios at Studebaker, which looked very European even if they weren't pure sports cars. But the independents were simply too strapped for money to compete with European sports cars head-on. They had to be more concerned with the higher-volume family models on which their profits and survival depended.

Chevrolet's Corvette, on the other hand, sprang from America's best-selling single make and the world's most successful car company, GM. Nevertheless, it was something of a hurry-up job, introduced as a Motorama showpiece in early '53 and rushed into limited production six months later. Power was provided by a low-suds six-cylinder engine mated to an uninspired two-speed automatic transmission, while unorthodox fiberglass body construction contrasted sharply with old-fashioned side curtains and a fairly rudimentary top.

With all this, the first Corvette was really more tourer than sports car. MG and Triumph fans were appalled by the trendy styling and unsporting automatic; those attracted to Eldorados and such didn't like the plastic side curtains and limited passenger and luggage space. By early 1954, GM was ready to drop the Corvette, but lobbying by design director Harley Earl and Chevy chief engineer Ed Cole won the car a reprieve—and further development. Corvette thus got its first V-8, the classic 265-cid Chevy small-block, for 1955,

followed by smooth new styling for '56, and optional fuel injection for 1957. The result was a true sports car that enjoyed increasing sales success into the Sixties and Seventies.

At Ford Motor Company's Dearborn headquarters, where GM's every move was carefully watched, the Corvette's arrival sparked a good deal of debate. Ford itself had been transformed from the disorganized company of 1945 into a dynamic competitor thanks to chairman Henry Ford II and president Ernest R. Breech. It was

traditional for Ford to respond to any GM initiative with one of its own. Should it now field a challenger to the low-volume plastic sports car?

According to former product planner Tom Case, "There wasn't any question about it. Mr. Ford wanted a civilized sports car, if we were going to build a two-seater at all. The Corvette was too spartan, too much like an MG. You just couldn't imagine Mr. Ford struggling to raise one of those plastic side curtains." Ford's reply duly appeared at the end of 1954: the Thunderbird.

Opposite page: Italy gave American sports-car drivers the Alfa Romeo Giulietta (*top*); Germany the Mercedes-Benz 190SL (*second from top*). The Nash-Healey (*third from top*) was an Anglo-American hybrid built in England but powered by the Nash Ambassador's overhead-valve six. American entries into the two-seater fray included the 1954 Kaiser-Darrin (*bottom*) and (*this page*) the 1955 Chevrolet Corvette (*top*), now with V-8 power, and the 1955 Thunderbird (*above*), which Ford wisely called a "personal" car.

This new steel-bodied two-seater was pushed into production by Henry Ford's lieutenant, Lewis D. Crusoe, general manager of Ford Division. Crusoe was a marketing man first, a car buff second, and the Thunderbird reflected this in being primarily a marketing maneuver designed to outflank Chevrolet. From the start, Crusoe decreed that it would be V-8 powered; a six wouldn't even be offered. The engine chosen was a 292-cubic-inch Mercury unit with close to 200 bhp. Crusoe also mandated automatic transmission and a bolt-on hardtop as options. A deluxe interior complete with conventional roll-up windows was also planned from the start. Styling, largely the work of Robert Maguire, Damon Woods, and Bill Boyer under the supervision of Frank Hershey, was spectacular: sporty yet elegant and recognizably Ford.

At $2944, the T-Bird was price-competitive with the new V-8 Corvette. But given buyer preference for luxury features, the outcome of the '55 sales fight was predictable. While Chevrolet moved a mere 674 Corvettes, Ford sold 16,155 Thunderbirds. After a mild facelift and 15,631 sales, the T-Bird was more extensively reworked for '57, gaining a combination bumper/grille, modest tailfins, revised interior, and a wider choice of engines with horsepower as high as 300. Sales rose to 21,380.

But even as the first two-seat T-Bird rolled off the line, an all-new four-seat replacement was being prepared for 1958. The marketing decisions that led to this are crucial to the Mustang story for, as Tom Case observed, "The Mustang was really the original Thunderbird revived—with two extra seats."

The change came after Crusoe moved up in the company hierarchy. Replacing him as Ford Division general manager was Robert S. McNamara, one of the "Whiz Kids" that young Henry Ford II had recruited after taking over the company reins from his legendary grandfather. McNamara, a no-nonsense type (he would be President Kennedy's Secretary of Defense, then president of the World Bank), decided that Ford Motor Company would no longer build cars just for the sake of image. From now on, every Ford product would be designed mainly to make money.

The effects of this policy reached far beyond Ford Division, and McNamara was

soon exerting considerable influence on top corporate management. For example, a Mercury production expert was brought in at his behest to make recommendations on how the exclusive Continental Mark II could be built and sold more profitably. The Mark II had been Ford's ultimate car in 1956-57, but the company lost about $1000 on every one it sold despite a lofty $10,000 price. Under McNamara's direction, the replacement Mark III was designed to share components with the higher volume 1958 Lincoln. The result was a far less distinctive car, but one that was much cheaper to build. For the first time, the Continental made a profit.

Making money was even more important at Ford Division, aside from its perennial rivalry with Chevrolet. Accordingly, McNamara ditched the flashy but slow-selling 1955-56 Crown Victoria, which featured an optional—and costly—transparent plastic roof. The novel Skyliner, a convertible with a retractable steel roof instead of a folding cloth top, was already in the design stage when McNamara became division chief, and he was too late to stop it for 1957. But when it failed to sell in significant numbers for three successive seasons, he summarily axed it.

As for the Thunderbird, McNamara had three options. He could continue with a two-seater as a prestige item, selling it at a loss or perhaps a small profit; he could drop it entirely; or he could remake the

T-Bird into something that would sell in greater numbers than the two-seater promised. Given his orientation, the choice was obvious, and a four-seat model got the green light for 1958. Stylist Bill Boyer and others wanted to continue the two-seater as a companion model, but McNamara adamantly refused, feeling it would divert attention from the new, larger car, which would need to have maximum impact to stimulate initial sales.

Even before the decision was made to drop it, the two-seat Thunderbird had been a car of vastly different character compared with the Corvette. It was not a race-and-ride sports car, which the Corvette definitely *was* after 1955; it was, rather, a *boulevardier*. It looked sporty, but handled with little more agility than a standard Ford Fairlane, and was rarely seen in competition, where it wasn't very successful anyway. But it handily outsold Corvette by combining sports-car allure with the special styling and luxury of the early-postwar limited editions. Even so, the two-seater's annual sales of 15,000-20,000 units was too low for McNamara. The four-

Ford fielded the $10,000 Continental Mark II (*opposite*) in 1956 to outdo Cadillac—and even Rolls-Royce—at the very top end of the market. Ford also debuted new body styles in the Fifties, such as the "bubbletop" '56 Ford Crown Victoria Skyliner.

Although other cars had hinted at what would become the "personal-luxury" segment, it was the 1958 Ford Thunderbird, here a '59 (*this page*), that really blew it wide open and defined the requisite features: low and lithe, modest wheelbase, bucket-seat-and-console interior, and plenty of luxury features. The Chrysler 300, here a '59 300E (*opposite*), was also luxurious, but put the emphasis on all-out performance.

seater would have to triple or quadruple that rate to earn a permanent place in the line.

But McNamara knew what he was doing, and the 1958 Thunderbird was a sweeping sales success. Boasting a newly designed unit body and a low, ground-hugging stance, it was offered as a convertible and as a new fixed-roof hardtop with a handsome, wide-quarter roofline destined to be imitated by other Fords—

and other makes. To make up for its added weight compared with the "little Birds," the four-seater had a more powerful, 300-bhp 352-cid V-8 standard. Production was around 40,000 units for '58, the vast majority being hardtops; by 1960 the total was over 90,000. After 1963, the T-Bird was more luxury car than grand tourer, but it never lost the personal-luxury cachet established by the '58 "Squarebird." That image had strong appeal for many cus-

tomers who would never have been satisfied with a two-seater.

Unlike the limited editions and other personal cars before it, the four-seat Thunderbird was fresh from the ground up, created specifically for its market. It was intended not just to build showroom traffic but to sell in high volume. Its success was not lost on the competition. Chrysler soon added four bucket seats and a center console to its high-performance "letter-

series" 300s. A bit later, General Motors launched a squadron of personal or performance models from its various divisions, beginning with the luxurious, bucket-seat 1961 Oldsmobile Starfire convertible. Save Cadillac's Eldorado Brougham, however, none of these was really a separate model in its own right or a direct T-Bird competitor. It wasn't until 1963 that GM responded with the elegant Buick Riviera, conceived expressly by styling chief William L. Mitchell with the Thunderbird in mind.

Studebaker also emulated the Thunderbird package with its handsome 1962-64 Gran Turismo Hawk, a clever makeover of the firm's then nearly 10-year-old hardtop bodyshell by designer Brooks Stevens. Bearing a roofline obviously inspired by the Thunderbird's, the GT Hawk could be equipped with four-speed

gearbox, disc brakes and, after '62, even a supercharged V-8. But Studebaker was in dire financial straits, and the Hawk did not sell as well as it deserved—or well enough to help turn Studebaker around.

By that time, however, the four-seat T-Bird's swift, solid sales success and continuing buyer interest in sports cars suggested a new idea: the sporty, low-priced compact. First out was the Corvair Monza, arriving late in the 1960 model year as a trim option for Chevrolet's new rear-engine economy car. The most advanced of the Big Three compacts, Corvair was simply

The '61 Oldsmobile Starfire and the '63 Buick Riviera (*opposite, top and bottom*) were responses to the '58 T-Bird. The '57 Studebaker Golden Hawk (*below*) preceded it. The Corvair Monza (*right*) created a new market.

too unconventional as an economy car and did not sell well against Ford's ultra-simple Falcon. Chevy realized its mistake after two years of disappointing Corvair sales and brought out the front-engine, live-axle Chevy II to compete with Falcon. But with its vinyl bucket seats, full carpeting, and snazzy good looks, the Monza was seen by some as sort of a poor man's Porsche—or Thunderbird—and it sold like hotcakes. Priced at about $2200, it cost $1500 less than a T-Bird and some $500 less than a Triumph TR3. Successful beyond even GM's projections, the Monza would almost singlehandedly keep Corvair alive for the next nine years.

For 1961, Chevy offered an optional four-speed gearbox, which only added to the Monza's appeal. Compared with about 12,000 units for abbreviated 1960, Monza production soared to 143,000. Body style choices expanded for '62, including a new convertible, and sales shot up past 200,000. For the really serious driver there was the 150-bhp turbocharged Monza Spyder, another new '62 arrival that evolved into the 1965-66 Corsa. Spyders and Corsas were rapid, good-handling cars of a size and character Chevrolet had never built before. And over a winding road, a well-driven Spyder could give fits to an MG driver.

So the Corvair ultimately succeeded not as the economy car Chevy had planned

but as a sporty, fun-to-drive compact. Even more important, though, it revealed the existence of a brand-new market. Quite naturally, Monza was not alone for long. For 1962, Chrysler jumped into the fray with bucket-seat versions of its compact Plymouth Valiant and Dodge Lancer. That same year also saw the Chrysler Windsor

The '62 Ford Falcon Futura (*opposite*) featured bucket seats and an optional four-on-the-floor, but wasn't nearly as sporty as the Corvair Monza. The '67 Chevy II Nova SS, however, was a mover when equipped with the 327 V-8, as is the car shown (*above*).

replaced by a sportier "non-letter" 300 series. Priced at around $3500, it sold well by combining a milder, though still powerful, engine with the styling of the legendary letter series.

But public interest and the sales battles centered mainly on the sporty compacts. Rival GM divisions quickly followed Chevy's lead with the Buick Special Skylark, Pontiac Tempest Le Mans, and Oldsmobile F-85 Cutlass. Studebaker chimed in with the Lark Daytona for '62, offering the obligatory bucket seats plus complete instrumentation and options like disc brakes, four-speed gearbox, and performance V-8s of up to 300 bhp.

Ford Motor Company wasn't about to be left out of this money-making picture. Its first reply to Monza was the Falcon Futura, a spiffed-up two-door sedan arriving in the spring of 1961 with bucket seats and deluxe trim. It sold well and continued with few changes through 1963. More exciting was the Sprint, first offered in the spring of that year in convertible or hardtop form as a special version of the Futura. It was available with what would turn out to be a significant new engine: Ford's 260-cid small-block V-8 with 164 bhp. This powerful, efficient engine coupled to an optional four-speed gearbox made for truly vivid performance. And the Sprint offered all the features synonymous with performance in the Sixties: bucket seats, console, and extra instruments, including a 6000-rpm tachometer.

The Sprint continued through the Falcon's first restyle for 1964 and the second for 1966, by which time the small-block was up to 289 cid. By 1967 there was a "Stage 2" engine with four-barrel carburetor and 225 bhp. Mercury's Falcon-based Comet S-22 and Cyclone were similar in concept and performance to the Futura and Futura Sprint.

But anyone could see by the sales figures that the bucket-seat Falcons and Comets weren't sufficiently competitive with the Monza. Whether it was because of Chevrolet's superior promotion or the Corvair's novel rear-engine layout and all-independent suspension, buyers weren't as attracted to Dearborn's offerings. Against 73,000 Futuras and S-22 Comets for 1963 and 118,000 for '64, Chevrolet cranked out a whopping 350,000 Monzas. If Ford was going to beat Chevy in this race, it

would need a brand-new product, one designed especially for its market, just like the four-seat Thunderbird had been.

It's important to note that Ford was in an ideal position to create such a car by the early Sixties. A succession of able managers since 1945 had pulled a backward company from the brink of financial ruin and built it into a mighty colossus. By 1952, Ford Motor Company had regained its traditional spot as the industry's number-two producer, pushing Chrysler back to third, and Ford Division had actually outproduced Chevrolet on several occasions in the years since. This sales growth continued into the next decade. In 1964, for example, Ford Division produced nearly 1.8 million cars, a figure then exceeded only by 1923 in the make's history.

The decision to launch a sporty new personal car—but by no means a limited-edition model—occurred in 1961. Yet it wouldn't have been possible without consistently strong sales up and down the corporate line. Had the 1961-64 Fords sold poorly—or had the company created another Edsel—we might not have seen the Mustang until 1968 or '69, if then.

One reason Ford Division did so well in these years was McNamara's successor as general manager. McNamara was an able leader, but he wasn't a "car guy." His replacement was: a hard-working salesman blessed with both astute business sense and an enthusiast's appreciation of automotive design. As everyone knows, that man was Lee Iacocca.

The '64 Monza Spyder (*opposite*) came equipped with a turbocharged 150-bhp version of the Corvair's flat six. It sold for $2811 as a convertible. Ford had upped the performance ante in 1963 with the Falcon Sprint (*below*), which came standard with a 260-cid, 164-bhp light-block V-8. It sold for $2320 as a hardtop, $2600 in convertible form, thus easily undercutting the Monza Spyder.

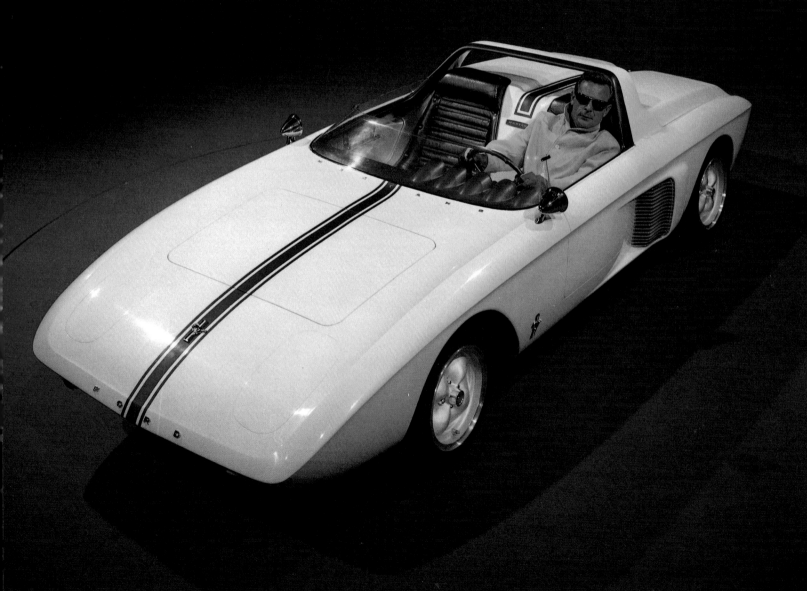

CHAPTER TWO

Designing a Legend: False Starts, a Fabulous Finish

The boss may not always be right, but he's always the boss. In Detroit, the boss may not always do the work, but he most always gets credit for it.

Take Lido Anthony Iacocca. Before his "second" career in the Eighties as chairman and chief saviour of Chrysler Corporation, Iacocca was widely regarded as the "father" of the greatest automotive success in postwar history. In truth, however, the Mustang was no more his personal creation than any of the numerous GM designs attributed to Harley Earl or Bill Mitchell. Major corporations and their projects are simply too big for any one person "to get their arms around," as Ed Cole once said of GM. Not that individual ideas don't count, but their end products, the ones we buy, most always result from teamwork—and fairly large teams, too.

The trouble is that with simplicity a virtue in storytelling, teams are not the stuff of which legends are made. This helps explain why corporate triumphs like the Mustang so often end up being inextricably linked to the one man or woman in charge, even though he or she may have merely approved what countless others spent countless hours to achieve.

It is perhaps more accurate to view Iacocca's role in the Mustang's birth as that of chief mover-and-shaker. As Ford Division general manager in 1961, when the sporty-compact idea first came up, he certainly had the means. That the idea itself was his alone is doubtful. As we've seen, it was suggested by market conditions in general and the instant popularity of Chevy's Corvair Monza in particular. But because of his position, Iacocca was quick to be credited as principal architect once the Mustang debuted—as *Time*, *Newsweek*, and similar mass media actually did—though others in Dearborn had surely been thinking along the same lines at the same time he had.

Nevertheless, as a sales-wise executive who's always been what we now call a "car guy," Iacocca couldn't help but leave his personal imprint on the original ponycar, though a great many others did, too, as we'll see. Yet because his input and decisions were crucial to the car's development, it's appropriate to look at Iacocca's career in the years leading up to the Mustang's genesis.

Lee's father, Nicola, had emigrated to America from southern Italy at the age of

12. As a teenager, he'd scraped together enough cash to buy a secondhand Model T, which he occasionally rented out to acquaintances in and around Allentown, Pennsylvania. Within eight years this business had blossomed into 33 cars, most of them Fords, and Nicola soon branched out into real estate. By the Depression, his family's holdings had reached a net worth of over a million dollars, a fortune they managed to keep largely intact through those hard times.

Wrote *Time* magazine in its 1964 cover story on Nicola's son at the time of the Mustang's introduction: "Lee Iacocca never wavered from early youth in his desire to go into the auto business—with Ford. For him, it was something like wanting to join the priesthood. 'I suppose it was partly because my father had always been greatly interested in automobiles,' he says, 'and because I was influenced by family friends who were Ford dealers.'"

Lee breezed through high school with excellent grades, earned his bachelor's degree at Lehigh University, then got a master's degree in mechanical engineering from Princeton on a scholarship. Next, he whizzed through an 18-month Ford marketing course in only half the time and, soon afterward, found himself with an offer to become a transmission engineer in Dearborn. Deciding that wasn't for him, he took a job at a tiny Ford sales outpost in Pennsylvania. He did exceedingly well, and began climbing the ladders of various regional sales offices.

In 1956, Iacocca came to the attention of Ford division chief Robert McNamara, who took a sales scheme Iacocca had

One of the earliest ideas for a sporty personal Ford was the Mustang I (*both pages*), a styling study created in 1962 with the help of engineer Herb Misch and styling chief Eugene Bordinat. Mustang I was a two-seater with all-independent suspension that had adjustable springs and shocks, tubular frame, and integral roll bar. The engine, a 60-degree V-4, displaced 1927 cc and produced 90 bhp.

37

dreamed up for Pennsylvania and applied it to the entire country. This was the "$56 a month for a '56 Ford" plan, and it worked. McNamara later said it helped sell an additional 72,000 cars. From there, promotions came thick and fast as the cigar-puffing Iacocca worked sales magic on most any car or truck he touched, even if

Ford didn't always build them the way he would have liked.

Iacocca had a habit of using little black notebooks to chart and plan his career. At one point, he wrote that he intended to become a Ford vice-president by age 35. Those black books soon became a topic of dinner conversation all over Dearborn.

One story told in those days concerned an incident where he'd run into flak from subordinates who resented so young a man telling them what to do. Iacocca reportedly passed out little black books to them, asking them to write down what they expected to accomplish over the next few years and in what order. Then, every three

months, Iacocca would grade his staff against their own goals. When some older hands started grousing about this, he told them, "Get with it. You're being observed. Guys who don't get with it don't play on the club after awhile." Sniffed one staffer, "He really knows how to whipsaw his men with that notebook."

That 35th birthday came and went without a vice-presidency. Iacocca later confessed to *Newsweek* that he was so disappointed that he thought to himself, "Hell, that's the end." But 18 days later, Henry Ford II offered him a vice-presidency. A year after that, in 1960, Iacocca took McNamara's place as Ford Division general manager.

Ford styling was always busy trying new design concepts. Among them were the Avanti or Median, later called Avventura in 1961-62 (*opposite, top*), and which was later evolved into the Allegro II (*bottom*). *This page*: Some 13 styling studies went under the Allegro name; the two seen here were dated June and July, 1962.

The Mustang was an entry in Iacocca's personal black book, reflecting his hunch that there must be a market looking for a sporty, low-cost compact. That hunch was backed up by several important facts. For one thing, Ford was still getting letters from people who missed the "personal" character of the two-seat Thunderbird and wanted either a revival or something very much like it. Chevrolet, meantime, was enjoying an unexpected mini-bonanza in the Corvair Monza, and sales of imported sports cars like Jaguar, MG, Triumph, and Austin-Healey had risen to a brisk 80,000 units a year despite fairly high prices. Also relatively expensive, but much admired and talked about, were Chevy's Corvette and the letter-series Chrysler 300s. Iacocca

reasoned that if the flashiness and performance of these costlier cars could be stuffed into an inexpensive car for the masses, it would sell like crazy.

It was the glint of a trend, and Iacocca had scribbled it down in his black book. He was thinking of a car he himself might want, though it was still pretty hazy in early 1961. It didn't have a name, of course, nor was it defined as having two seats or four; a front, rear, or central engine location; or a metal or fiberglass body. Those decisions would come in due time.

For the moment, Iacocca was still trying to change the somewhat lackluster image Ford Division cars had acquired under McNamara. A good administrator, McNamara had left the division in beautiful

financial shape, but his steadfast refusal to build anything—no matter how exciting —if it didn't sell in high volume had cost Ford the sporty image it had begun to acquire with the two-seat Thunderbird. *Time* magazine commented that his cars were "...like McNamara himself, [with] rimless glasses and hair parted in the middle."

Both pages: Convertibles and notchback and fastback coupes were all included in Allegro design studies done in 1962. The long-hood, short-deck styling that became an industry standard in the mid-1960s was an integral part of the look being considered. Some of the ideas tried are probably best left forgotten.

9-7-62
S-5684-8 9A

8-16-62
S-5639-4

8-16-62
S-5639-2

Once installed as general manager, Iacocca started sprucing things up. He arrived too late to do much about the 1961-62 line, but he was able to get out some considerably jazzier offerings for mid-year 1962 and again for "1963½." (The mid-year introduction, just before the start of the spring selling season, was already a favorite Iacocca marketing technique.) It was Iacocca who approved dropping a

V-8 into the Falcon, okayed fastback roofs for some big Fords, and plunged the division back into racing in a big way. With the blessing of Henry Ford II, Dearborn reentered NASCAR competition and was very successful on the big Southern tracks. By 1965, Ford had also won Sebring and Indianapolis, and had almost won Le Mans. It was all part of Iacocca's "thinking young."

Iacocca first broached the subject of a youth-oriented sporty car at a 1961 meeting of the Fairlane Group, an informal eight-man committee comprising top Ford executives and representatives from the division's ad agency. The group got its name from the Fairlane Inn Motel on Michigan Avenue in Dearborn, where it met each week. This group decided the sporty-compact idea might be worth pur-

suing, which led to project T-5. (Production 1965 Mustangs would be sold in Germany under that designation.)

Two additional groups now became involved: market research, under the direction of marketing manager Chase Morsey, Jr., and a team of young engineers and designers headed by Donald N. Frey, who was Iacocca's product planning manager at the time. Market Research was

supposed to prove or disprove Iacocca's hunch. Product Planning's mission was to come up with a car to fill the market void—if indeed there was one.

Morsey's data yielded some very encouraging conclusions. First, the vast postwar baby boom generation was just reaching car-buying age in 1960. Further, the 15-29 age group would swell by about 40 percent between 1960 and 1970, while

By January 1963, design studies were beginning to look a lot like the Mustang that would ultimately emerge. *Top row:* The license plate says Falcon and the fender badges say Cougar on this clay mock-up, which explores a two-door pillared coupe body style on one side and a four-door sedan on the other. The convertible (*bottom row*) still bears Cougar badges a month later, but the license plate identifies it as a "Special."

the number of 30-39-year-olds would actually decrease by nine percent in the same period. Second, buyers between 18 and 34 were expected to account for more than half the projected increase in new-car sales in 1960-70.

Third, research showed that car styling in the Sixties would need to reflect the preferences and tastes of younger buyers, not the older generations. And the study concluded that young people had clear ideas about styling and performance: "...36 percent of all persons under 25 liked the 'four on the floor' feature. Among those over 25, only nine percent wanted to shift gears. Bucket seats were a favorite feature among 35 percent of young people, as against 13 percent in the older groups..." Fourth, buyers were becoming more educated, sophisticated, and willing to spend cash for what the study termed "image extensions."

Finally, more families would have more money, the number with incomes above $10,000 expected to rise by a whopping 156 percent between 1960 and 1975. Thus, more households would be able to afford second and even third or fourth cars. Women and teenagers were the family members who wanted cars of their own.

So a potential and sizable market definitely existed. It was a young, affluent

group, and big enough to represent substantial potential demand for the right kind of new car—something distinctive and sporty, but not too expensive. The question faced by the T-5 planners was, what should that car be?

One of the first alternatives considered was the mid-engine Mustang I, an experimental two-seat sports car aimed more at the Triumph/MG market than the Corvette/Jaguar class. It was the product of an inspired triumvirate; an engineer, a stylist, and a product planner. The engineer was Herb Misch, who'd come to Dearborn from Packard when former Studebaker-

Clay mock-up dubbed Torino (*above*) incorporates appearance features from the production Mustang, like side scoops and three-part taillights. In the fall of '63, a running prototype called Mustang II (*bottom row*) was shown around the country, beginning at Watkins Glen. Few realized then that it was a sneak preview. A late production prototype (*right*) still sports a Cougar in the grille.

Packard president James Nance was named to head Edsel Division. The stylist was Eugene Bordinat. The product planner was Roy Lunn, formerly of Aston Martin and later a member of Ford's Product Study Vehicles Department. It was Lunn who laid out the basic design.

Because it seemed necessary to start from the ground up, Mustang I was carefully considered. As a challenger to Triumph and MG, it was planned around a wheelbase of 85-90 inches and an engine of 1.5-2.0 liters, mounted behind the cockpit and ahead of the rear-wheel centerline in a multi-tubular frame covered by an aluminum body. Since it was impossible to complete a prototype very rapidly in Detroit, Ford contracted the job to specialist builder Trautman and Barnes in Los Angeles. T&B also built the frame, from one-inch steel tubing. The stressed-skin body comprised separate aluminum panels only .06-inch thick, with an integral roll bar and fixed seats for added rigidity. Though the seats didn't adjust, pedals and steering wheel did, the former mounting on a sliding box-member.

Lunn and Misch devised the Mustang I's four-wheel independent suspension, then an uncommon feature in Detroit, land of the solid rear axle. Upper wishbones, lower triangulated arms, and radius rods were used at the rear, with widely spaced attachment points so that stress would be evenly distributed throughout the structure. Up front were wishbones, splayed coil springs, and Monroe telescopic shocks. All shocks and springs were adjustable for ride height and firmness. Steering was by a rack-and-pinion unit similar to that of the prototype Ford Cardinal, which evolved into Germany's production Taunus 12M. The steering was geared to provide just 2.9 turns lock-to-lock and a tight 30-foot turning circle.

The Mustang I engine was derived from the powerplant developed for the Cardinal, a program begun in 1959 to design what we would now call a subcompact, a car smaller than Falcon to slot in below it in Ford's U.S. lineup. The Cardinal was unusual for its day in having front-wheel drive. Its engine was also unusual: a 60-degree V-4 displacing 1927 cc (90 × 60-mm bore and stroke). For the Mustang I it was tuned to produce 90 bhp at 6500 rpm, breathing through a small, single-throat Solex carburetor. A competition

version was also devised with two twin-throat sidedraft Weber carbs and crossover manifold, good for over 100 bhp.

Predicting the Pontiac Fiero and Toyota MR2 of 20 years later, the Cardinal's front-drive powertrain—engine and associated transaxle—were moved aft to drive to the Mustang I's rear wheels. The transaxle was a four-speed affair with cable-operated linkage and mated to a 7.5-inch-diameter clutch with special linings, adapted from the British Ford Consul. Gear ratios weren't particularly close (4.02, 2.53, 1.48, 1.00), but a 3.30:1 final drive made them suitable for the V-4.

The Mustang I followed contemporary sports car practice in having disc brakes at the front and drums at the rear. The parking brake operated on the rear drums, a less expensive proposition for mass production than one working on rear discs. The front discs, designed to take about 80 percent of total braking load, were 9.5-inch Girling units borrowed from the Ford Britain's 109E Anglia. Rolling stock comprised 13-inch magnesium wheels from Lotus of England shod with Pirelli radial-ply tires.

Dimensionally, the Mustang I measured 154 inches long overall, rode a 90-inch wheelbase, and spanned front/rear tracks of 48/49 inches. Careful construction resulted in a stated curb weight of less than 1200 pounds, which meant thrilling performance despite the small engine: Top

speed was approximately 115 mph. A low, sloping nose housing the spare tire left little space for a radiator and ductwork, so a pair of diagonally mounted radiators flanked the engine, one per side, each with a thermostatically controlled fan. The fuel tank was a 13-gallon aluminum-alloy reservoir with a racing-style "quick-fill" neck.

Under Bordinat's direction, Mustang I styling went from sketch to approved clay model in just 21 days. Thanks to Lunn, the car met *Federation Internationale de l'Automobile* (FIA) and Sports Car Club of America (SCCA) racing regulations. Even its roll bar was SCCA-legal. So was its cut-down racing windshield, though a

conventional full screen was developed for road use. There was no soft top, but a light folding hardtop attaching to the header of the full windshield was also designed with an eye to production. Concern for good aerodynamics dictated retracting headlights to keep the nose as low as possible, and even a fold-away front license plate mount. And though it *was* low—less than 40 inches high—the Mustang I had nearly five inches of ground clearance.

Interior styling was another rush job by the Ford studio, but nicely executed. The instrument panel was a slim, five-pod design presenting fuel gauge, speedometer, tachometer, ammeter, and coolant temperature gauge. Ignition and light switches

47

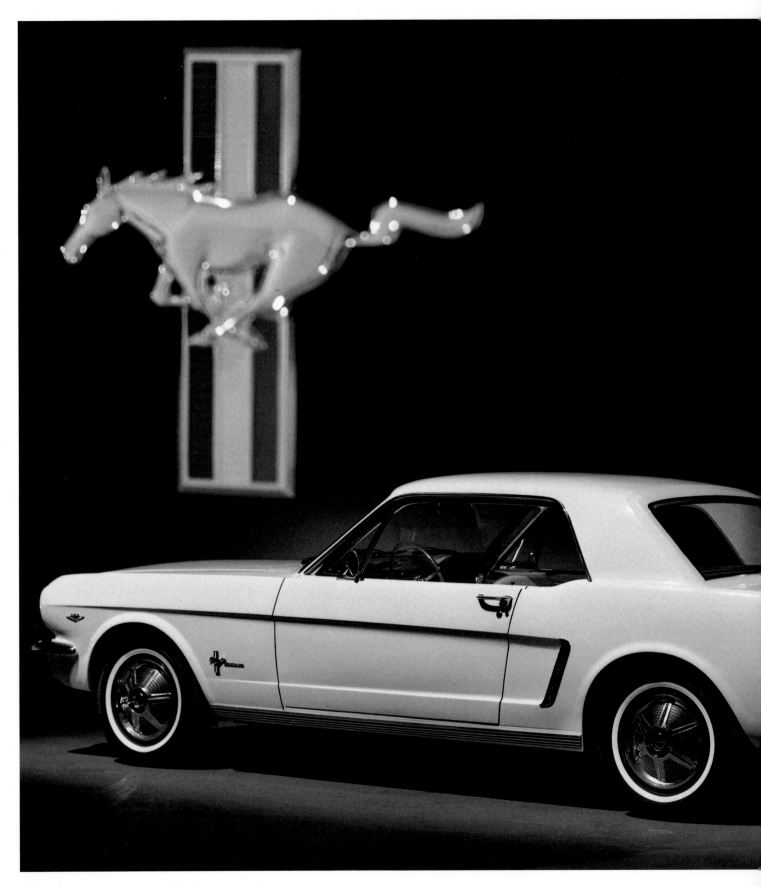

mounted in an angled extension of the driver's armrest, and a passenger grab handle hung down on the dashboard's far right. The choke and horn button lived on a central console alongside the shifter and pull-up handbrake. A rubber mat covered the floor. In all, the Mustang I cockpit was stark but practical and functional, in keeping with the goal of low production cost.

The Mustang I made its public debut at the United States Grand Prix at Watkins Glen, New York, in October 1962, where it was driven around the circuit to the cheers of fans by race driver Dan Gurney. *Car and Driver* later tested the car in 90-bhp form and found it as fast as Ford claimed. Its 0-60-mph acceleration was about 10 seconds, yet fuel economy was as high as 30 miles per gallon.

As expected of mid-engine cars, handling was excellent. The Mustang I "reminds us of the first two-seat 1100-cc Coventry Climax-engined Cooper more than any other car," *C/D*, enthused, "and the Mustang seemed more forgiving. It can be braked well into a turn, and with power on its stability is striking." The magazine also praised the beautifully precise rack-and-pinion steering, but felt body modifications would be needed to provide adequate luggage space and that electric motors were a must for the retractable lights; on the prototype the driver had to get out and hand-crank them into position.

Innovative and exciting though it was, the Mustang I was a false start. While Ford engineers and stylists, Dan Gurney, and sports-car lovers raved, Iacocca carefully watched general reaction—and shrugged. "All the buffs said, hey what a car! It'll be the best car ever built," he later observed. "But when I look at the guys saying it—the offbeat crowd, the *real* buffs—I said that's sure not the car we want to build, because it can't be a volume car. It's too far out."

Iacocca's conclusion may have been affected by a prior decision on the Cardinal project. Cost estimates had indicated that the front-drive subcompact would have been only marginally profitable against the VW Beetle and other small imports. It was thus decided to build the Cardinal in Europe but not the United States. This effectively ended hopes for a production Mustang I, which was designed to share major mechanical components with the

high-volume Cardinal and would have been economically feasible if that car were built here. Without a U.S. Cardinal to borrow parts from, the Mustang I would have been costly to build, and Iacocca realized that with the high resulting retail price, it just wouldn't generate enough sales volume to offset its steep tooling and development expenses.

Similar drawbacks plagued another early-Sixties two-seat proposal, the Falcon-based XT-Bird. This was an exercise in production engineering by the Budd Body Company, a long-time Ford supplier, at about the time Mustang I was being developed. Budd had built the original 1955-57 Thunderbird bodies, and still had the dies. The firm's engineers concluded that this tooling could be utilized for a new production car combining the chassis and drivetrain of the 1961 Falcon with a modified version of the '57 T-Bird body-shell.

A prototype was duly run up on a Falcon chassis, with much of its underbody structure intact. Styling was updated by shearing off the '57 tailfins and lowering the front fenders, and Budd ingeniously managed to retain the original dashboard and cowl. In deference to contemporary tastes, the wrapped windshield and its severe dogleg gave way to less angled A-pillars, and front quarter vents were added. Like the '57, the XT-Bird had a steel body with a soft top that folded down into a well ahead of the decklid. Unlike the original, it had a small rear jump seat that could either carry children or be folded down into a luggage platform.

Knowing Iacocca was seeking a new image-builder, Budd executives went out of their way to interest Ford in the XT-Bird. They pointed to the extraordinarily high resale value of 1955-57 Thunderbirds as suggesting a strong, unmet buyer demand for their updated version. Adapting the old dies would enable Ford to keep list price attractively low, Budd estimating the finished production model could retail for around $2800. "The total tool, jig, and fixture costs...would not exceed $1.5

Another shot of the car seen on pages 46-47 emphasizes the Mustang crest, which features a lively pony galloping across an all-American red, white, and blue background.

million," Budd wrote. "We could ship the entire body-in-white...for a total unit cost of between $350 and $400...We believe that we could be shipping complete bodies-in-white for this car six months from the day you authorize us to start on the job." Such low production and development costs were an accountant's dream.

In the end, though, the XT-Bird was only wishful thinking. Lack of full four-passenger capacity was its main limitation, though dumpy lines didn't help.

The Fairlane Group also passed over two other two-seat designs; an open racer called Median and a sports model called Mina. By 1962, dozens of four-seat packages—paper renderings and quarter- and full-scale clays—had been designed. After reviewing them all, management asked that one, a four-seater dubbed "median sports car," be worked up into a coupe and convertible, feeling that its styling captured some of the original T-Bird's personal flavor. It was also mocked-up as a two-seater, a 2+2 with jump seats, and a 2+2 with a set of cramped rear bucket seats.

This exercise led to another round of studies under the name Avventura, a dozen different clay models. One of these became the Allegro X-car, publicly shown in August 1963. Actually there were 13 Allegros, each differing slightly in dimensions and interior packaging. Ford as much as admitted that none would ever be produced by labeling Allegro a "styling experimental car."

The Allegro was built on a 99-inch wheelbase, stood 50 inches high, stretched 63.5 inches wide, and was 170 inches long. These dimensions were chosen partly to accommodate the Falcon's 144-cid overhead-valve six, which mandated a conventional drivetrain layout: a front-mounted engine ahead of a manual transmission connected by driveshaft to a live rear axle.

For cost reasons, Ford was leaning more and more toward drivetrain components

shared with one of its American-made cars, though it stated that the Allegro "could accommodate the 170-cubic-inch [Falcon] six or the 1200-cc or 1500-cc V-4s of the [German Ford] Taunus with its front-wheel drive." Had the V-4 and fwd arrangements been used, noted *Road & Track* magazine, "it would seem that there is space for four passengers without major body alterations, and the width of the door (for rear seat entrance) bears this out."

As in Mustang I, the Allegro's seats were fixed and pedals movable to fit the driver. The steering wheel also adjusted, up and down, and even swung out of the way as on contemporary production Thunder-birds; a "memory button" returned it to a preset position once the driver was seated. Also featured were retractable seatbelts, a portent of the future. Because the seats were fixed structural elements, the belts were attached directly to them, reflecting aircraft design influence.

The Allegro and its many variations occupied Ford management for about a year, until mid-summer 1962. But by that time, the theme had been worked to death and was stale. Accordingly, Bordinat, Frey, Iacocca, Henry Ford II, and their associates decided in August to start over with a new series of clays. Another set of dimensions was laid down, and four styling teams were invited to submit proposals to fit. Specifications now called for a target price of $2500, a 2500-pound curb weight, a 180-inch maximum overall length, four seats, floorshift, and the use of mostly Falcon mechanicals. Styling character would be "sporty, personal and tight." Finally, Ford tossed in a marketing brain-storm, probably the key to the entire concept: an arm-long option list that would let the buyer tailor the car for economy, luxury, performance, or any combination.

Four studios went to work, representing Ford and Lincoln-Mercury Divisions, Corporate Projects, and Advanced Design. All, of course, were guided by Bordinat, who gave them just two weeks to come up with suitable clays. Seven were ultimately submitted, and on August 16 they were gathered in the Ford Design Center's outdoor viewing area for management perusal. One leaped out from the rest. "It was the only one in the courtyard that seemed to be moving," Iacocca said later. Henry Ford II agreed.

This came from the Ford Division studio under Joe Oros (later executive director of Ford and Lincoln-Mercury design), studio manager Gail Halderman, and executive designer L. David Ash. The group had talked about the assignment at length before anyone even put pencil to paper. "We said what we would and wouldn't do," said Oros. "We didn't want the car to look like any other car. It had to be unique." They talked so much, in fact, that once they started, they needed only three days to draw the shape that so impressed Iacocca.

It looked very much like the eventual production Mustang, but lacked a front bumper and wore Cougar emblems, though the name was changed to Torino, then Turino as development work progressed. Finally, and confusingly, it was labelled Mustang II. Oros deliberately painted the clay white so it would stand out at the showing and increase his team's chances of winning the intramural competition. Judging from the reaction of Iacocca and HF II, that tactic—and the styling—succeeded handsomely.

Like the Budd XT-Bird, the Cougar/Torino/Mustang II was designed around the Falcon floorpan, though the Oros team planned for drivetrains up to and including the 289-cid, 271-bhp V-8 and four-speed all-synchromesh transmission from Ford's mid-size Fairlane. To provide true four-passenger seating, wheelbase was pegged at 108 inches, only 1.5 inches shorter than the Falcon's. Track was 56 inches front and rear. Overall length was 186.6 inches, a bit more than the specified maximum.

In 1963, a running prototype based on the Oros design and also called Mustang II was built and displayed around the country. Like Mustang I, it was first shown at Watkins Glen, before the U.S. Grand Prix. Though no one knew it at the time, this was actually a sneak preview of Ford's forthcoming sporty compact. Iacocca had indicated earlier that if Ford was going to mass-produce such a car, Mustang II had the best chance among any of the experimentals seen to date. "Our preliminary studies," he said, "indicate that a car of this type could be built in this country to sell at a price of under $3000."

Meanwhile, Oros and company had one more fling with a two-seater. Called Cougar II, this running prototype, shown in late 1963 and early '64, was a fastback coupe with exciting lines not unlike those of the 1963 Corvette Sting Ray split-window coupe. And though Ford didn't mention it, the Cougar II was dimensionally quite close to the rip-snorting A.C. Cobra: 90-inch wheelbase, front/rear track of 50.5/52 inches, 66.5-inch width, 48-inch height; 168-inch overall length. Chassis features included the Fairlane 260 V-8, four-speed all-synchromesh gearbox, and all-

Early publicity shots and ads almost always featured a white Mustang, often with the low $2368 base price prominently displayed. Engineering of the car was totally conventional, but the styling caught on immediately.

independent suspension. Said *Road & Track*: "The aerodynamics look reasonably good and the performance should be excellent, especially with one of the hotter versions of the Cobra-ized Fairlane V-8."

Anticipating a future Corvette feature, the Cougar II had a removable roof panel. It was a good idea, providing closed GT comfort with a measure of convertible openness. But it was discovered the rear roof/backlight acted as an air scoop with the panel removed, which apparently benefitted aerodynamics somewhat but also had an unexpected side effect — a blown-out rear window. Oros later added a "relief panel" vent behind the seats that opened when pressure against the backlight reached 15 pounds per square inch.

The Cougar II was certainly the closest thing to a genuine street sports car yet seen from Dearborn (not counting Carroll Shelby's Ford-powered, British-built Cobra), with the smoothest styling of any of the personal-car prototypes developed in these years. But it suffered the same problem that weighed against the Mustang I and XT-Bird: Ford just didn't think a two-seater would sell in sufficient numbers to assure a satisfactory return on tooling costs. Also, the Cougar II didn't fit Iacocca's idea for a low-cost four-seater, and its styling was probably too close to the Sting Ray's to suit many in Dearborn.

On September 10, 1962, the original white Cougar clay model that had wowed the company brass a few weeks earlier was "validated" for production. Only now did Ford Engineering get involved. This was unusual, because engineers are typically called in at a much earlier stage in a vehicle's development than was the case with the Mustang. The need to keep styling options open was probably the reason. Said Jack J. Prendergast, executive engineer for light vehicles: "Styling kept the engineers out too long, but even so, Engineering and Styling worked together very smoothly." Except for routine compromises needed to adapt a styling prototype for mass production (conventional bumpers, round headlights, a less rakish windshield), the Oros design saw relatively few changes. Engineering bent over backward, in fact, to keep the styling intact.

The Mustang was mainly a body engineering job, because its basic chassis, engine, suspension, and driveline were, by design, off-the-shelf Falcon and Fairlane components. At 181.6 inches, its overall length was identical to the 1964 Falcon's. Wheelbase, at 108 inches, remained 1.5 inches shorter. The Mustang might have shared some Falcon sheetmetal, too, but that idea didn't last long.

Studio manager Gail Halderman recalls having to "bend something like 78 Ford Motor Company in-house standards or rules in order to build this car." He was referring to a rulebook used by Ford designers at that time, listing specific do's and don'ts for production body engineering. Among other things, the eventual Mustang's radical rear-fender tuckunder, minimal bumper-to-sheetmetal clearance, die-cast headlight bezels, and the degree of roll-under for its front bumper pan were all prohibited. Where Engineering couldn't make structural pieces fit Styling's lines and curves (as with the front pan, where there was no room for bumper bracing), the design was revised as little as possible.

Though the notchback hardtop would always be the best-selling Mustang body style, Ford was still playing around with two-seaters and other variations of the new sporty compact. One particularly interesting "two-sided" mockup appears in a series of Design Center photos dated January 7, 1963. On the left it's the basic Oros hardtop in near final form, while the right is configured as a pillared four-door sedan with a T-Bird-style wide-quarter roofline. The semi-fastback coupe that would be added at the start of the formal 1965 model year was more or less complete by December '63. Most intriguing of all was a full-scale two-seat version of the production Mustang convertible, apparently built on a shortened wheelbase and photographed in the Design Center courtyard in June 1964, some two months after the production Mustang's splashy public debut.

Save the fastback, such "line extensions" ultimately came to nought, but they showed that at least some Ford designers just couldn't resist seeing how the racy Mustang styling would work on more prosaic body types. Their fascination continued to be evident in stillborn proposals for later styling generations, up to and including the 1971-73 design. Among these experiments were a sleek two-door "sportwagon" (a late-1966 idea for the '69 line), a targa-top convertible, and a fast-roof hatchback coupe.

The many optional engines and different horsepower ratings contemplated for the Mustang made a rigid base essential. Prendergast recalls that "the platform-type frame, evolved from previous light-car experience, was designed to be really in the middle. All the various chassis components were attached to the underside, and all the body components were installed topside." Heavy box-section side rails with five welded-in crossmembers formed the base. The convertible used heavier-gauge steel and extra reinforcements in the rocker areas. The frames of the first coupes were so stiff that they actually resonated, and were accordingly softened a bit.

Prendergast also observed that at the time the Mustang was being readied for production, Engineering had learned quite a bit about noise, vibration, and harshness (NVH) through experience with the Falcon and Comet. The result was better engineering solutions for certain problems, such as choice of suspension components, than on those earlier cars. The Mustang suspension, in fact, drew heavily from the later Falcon Sprint/Comet Caliente/Fairlane family. A running change made to the 1964 versions of these cars anticipated the ponycar's arrival. Because of the Mustang's low hoodline, engineers lowered the air cleaner and countersunk the radiator filler cap on Falcons, Comets, and Fairlanes, components Mustang would share. In a similar way, all Mustang mechanical parts were in production and even catalogued several months before the car itself debuted.

There was still the problem of finding a suitable name. Although "Mustang" had been seriously considered early on, as shown by the mid-engine two-seater, it didn't take hold for some time. Different departments had applied a variety of working titles to the project which, logically enough, was known as "Special Falcon" for a time. Henry Ford II favored "T-Bird II"

Ford designers experimented with a variety of Mustang configurations, including a 4-door sedan. One of the more interesting was this 2-seat convertible, which was built on a wheelbase several inches shorter than the production car's. The stillborn study was photographed in the courtyard of Ford's Design Center.

or "Thunderbird II." Surprisingly, Iacocca had no strong preference.

To get some additional ideas, John Conley of Ford's ad agency was dispatched to the Detroit Public Library. Earlier, he'd combed through lists of bird names to come up with Falcon for Ford's 1960 compact. (Chrysler, he later learned, had already used it on a 1955 experimental sports car, but a friendly phone call from Henry Ford II netted him the rights to it.) This time, Conley was interested in horses, considering Colt, Bronco, Pinto, and Maverick. All four would eventually be seen on cars: Colt by Dodge; Bronco,

Pinto, and Maverick by Ford, of course.

Mustang, however, soon became the clear choice. In many ways it was a natural. It conjured up visions of cowboys, prairies, movie adventures, and the romantic West. It was easy to spell and easy to remember. As one Ford ad man said, "It had the excitement of the wide-open spaces, and it was American as all hell." Thus, the wild, free-spirited horse of the Western plains was carved out of mahogany as a template for the soon-to-be familiar chrome sculpture that graced the first production prototype. The Mustang was ready. A revolution was about to begin.

This page: The grille in this Mustang publicity shot does not show the horizontal bars in the grille, making it an early photo. *Opposite page*: This photo groups together (*from the foreground*) the Mustang I and Mustang II one-offs, the production '65 hardtop, and the Shelby GT-350. The last was practically race-ready right off the showroom floor.

CHAPTER THREE

1965-66:
Hi Yo,
Ponycar!

Mustang's introduction was targeted for the opening of the New York World's Fair on April 17, 1964. As if the public hadn't already been teased enough by a series of exciting show cars, Ford decided to tease it some more by "accidentally" baiting the press. On March 11, Henry Ford II's 20-year-old nephew, Walter Buhl Ford II, just "happened" to drive a black pre-production Mustang convertible to a luncheon in downtown Detroit. Fred Olmsted, auto editor for the Detroit *Free Press*, spotted it in a parking lot and hurriedly called photographer Ray Glonka. Glonka's picture was picked up by *Newsweek* and a number of other publications, giving the nation its first glimpse of the sporty new Ford, which only heightened public desire to see the car in full.

Time, meanwhile, had been following the Mustang's development in pictures, thanks to a deal with Ford. Photographer J. Edward Bailey had been with Oros and Bordinat almost since the beginning of the Mustang II clay. In return, the magazine had promised not to publish anything until introduction day. *Time* kept its word, but despite its hopes for an exclusive, *Newsweek* ran a cover story on Iacocca and his baby's birth the same week.

In fact, Ford publicists pulled off a rare feat: a barrage of media coverage in which *Life*, *Look*, *Esquire*, *U.S. News & World Report*, the *Wall Street Journal*, and most business and automotive publications carried big articles on Mustang just days before the official sales date. On the evening of April 16, Ford bought the 9 p.m. slot on all three television networks, and an estimated 29 million viewers were treated to the Mustang's unveiling without ever leaving their living rooms. The next morning, 2600 major newspapers carried announcement ads and articles.

In time-honored Detroit fashion, Ford invited some 150 auto editors to be its guests for the World's Fair opening and some sumptuous wining and dining. The next day, they were set loose in a herd of Mustangs for a drive to Motown. "These were virtually hand-built cars," recalls one Ford information officer. "Anything could have happened. Some of the reporters hotdogged these cars the whole way, and we were just praying they wouldn't crash or fall apart. Luckily everyone made it, but it was pure luck." The luck paid off with glowing reports in the weeks following.

Mustangs soon went on display in airport terminals, hotel lobbies, and dealer showrooms across the country. Base price was boldly advertised everywhere. And why not? At just $2368 f.o.b. Detroit for the hardtop, the Mustang was a tremendous bargain.

Predictably, public reaction was just as tremendous. One San Francisco trucker stared so hard at a Mustang sitting in a dealer's showroom that he drove right in through the window. A Chicago dealer had to lock his doors to keep people from crowding in and crushing his cars—and each other. A Pittsburgh agent made the mistake of hoisting his only Mustang on a lube rack; crowds pressed in so thick and fast that he couldn't get the car down until suppertime. One eastern dealership found itself with 15 customers wanting to buy the same Mustang, so the car was auctioned off; the winning bidder insisted on sleeping in it to be sure it wasn't sold out from under him before his check cleared the next morning.

It was the same story all over the land:

Everybody loved the Mustang. Dealers simply couldn't get them fast enough. All the early cars sold at or above retail, and with very unliberal trade-in allowances.

Long before all this, Ford had projected first-year Mustang sales at 100,000 units. As announcement day approached, Iacocca upped the estimate to 240,000 and switched his division's San Jose, California, plant to Mustang production. Iacocca had been conservative: It took only four months to sell 100,000 Mustangs. For the full 1965 model run—April 1964 through August 1965—a total of 680,989 were sold, an all-time industry record for first-year sales. By March 1966, the one-millionth Mustang had rolled off the line.

Mustang debuted on April 17, 1964, at the New York World's Fair. Two models were offered initially, a two-door hardtop and a soft top. Ford's new ponycar—although it wasn't called that yet—created quite a stir. Dealers were deluged with visitors—and firm orders.

A legend had been created overnight, and the years of effort and planning that had gone into its concept and design were a big part of that. Mustang proved to be right on target for a vast, hitherto untapped market. By almost any yardstick, it was the start of a revolution. The stampede was on.

Most automotive experts greeted the Mustang with qualified enthusiasm, which partly reflected the nature of the car. Underneath that striking new shape was little more than just another Detroit compact—and a humble Falcon at that. But most critics were willing to forgive this, because performance and handling equipment was available to make any Mustang a competent grand tourer. In fact, Ford's vast option list covered virtually every aspect of the car.

No surprise, then, that there has never really been a "typical" Mustang. Perhaps more than any car before it, the character of any particular one depended on how it was equipped. This chameleonlike ability to take on so many different personalities also accounts for the wide range of initial press reactions. So it's worth detailing early Mustang options, if only to indicate their variety and importance in the car's instant

The 1964 ½ Mustang ragtop listed at $2614. Buyers chose V-8s by a three-to-one margin, and they tended to load the cars with extras chosen from a long options list. The interior (*right*) featured bucket seats; a full-length console cost $51.50. The sparse dash borrowed heavily from the Falcon, but the $70.80 Rally-Pac added a steering-column-mounted tach and clock.

high appeal to such a wide range of customers.

Of course, it was precisely this broad appeal that made the car such a resounding success. Mustang took up the "personal" theme of its predecessors with an option list longer than anything Detroit had ever offered. For less than $3000 you could order a very individual, very exciting automobile—depending on whether you were willing to wait for your specially optioned dream to be built.

Standard equipment on the early "1964½" models included the 170-cubic-inch Falcon six, three-speed manual floorshift transmission, full wheel covers, padded dash, bucket seats, and carpeting. From there, you were on your own. A sampling: Cruise-O-Matic, four-speed manual or three-speed overdrive transmissions (around $180 depending on engine); three V-8s ($106-$328); limited-slip differential ($42); Rally-Pac (tachometer and clock, $69); power brakes ($42); front disc brakes (from late 1965 on, non-assisted, $58); power steering ($84); air conditioning (except with the "Hi-Performance" V-8); full-length center console ($50); deluxe steering wheel ($32); vinyl roof covering for the hardtop ($74); pushbutton AM radio with antenna ($58); knock-off-style wheel covers ($18 the set); 14-inch wire-wheel covers ($45) and styled-steel wheels (with V-8 only, $120); and a profusion of tires (including whitewalls and larger rubber up to 6.95 × 14).

There were also option *packages*: Visibility Group (mirrors and wipers, $36); Accent Group (pinstriping and rocker panel moldings, $27); special handling package (for V-8s only, $31); Instrument Group (needle gauges for fuel, water, oil pressure, and amperes, plus round speedometer, $109); and a GT Group (disc brakes, driving lights, and special trim, $165). The most expensive single option, air conditioning, listed at $283, and many of the more desirable individual items were well within the reach of most buyers.

Ford was still selling safety in 1964, though not nearly so loudly as it had since 1956, when it began hawking "Lifeguard Design" features like seatbelts and dashboard padding. But though you had to look hard to find them, you could order your Mustang with such praiseworthy add-ons as retractable seatbelts ($7 front only, $25 for a deluxe front/rear set), padded sunvisors ($6), and emergency flashers (also destined for Washington's required equipment list, $19).

One particular factory package is highly prized by today's collectors. This is the so-called "pony" interior, which Ford termed the Interior Decor Group. Priced at $107, it included the five-dial GT instrument cluster, woodgrain appliqués on dash and door panels, a simulated-wood-rim steering wheel with bright accents, door courtesy lights, and—the main attraction—unique duotone vinyl upholstery with a herd of running horses embossed on the upper seatbacks. Distinctly odd, in view of the bucket-seat emphasis, was the available full-width front bench with center armrest at $24.

If your budget was really tight and you wanted to wait a bit to splurge, some factory-installed options were also available at your friendly neighborhood Ford dealer, who offered a plethora of additional accessories. These included expected items like door-edge guards ($3), rocker moldings ($20), left-side spotlight ($30) and

Opposite page: Enthusiasts liked the styled steel wheels ($122.30) and the Challenger 271 "hi-po" 289 V-8, which at $442.60 included a handling package. *This page*: The two upper photos show that the shape of the 2+2 fastback was pretty well finalized by December 1963. The production version bowed on October 1, 1964.

backup lamps ($10), and a few that weren't: decklid luggage rack ($35), "Studio-Sonic" reverberation unit ($23), left remote-control door mirror ($13), a matching right mirror (a mere $7), remote trunk release (take *that*, Japan, $7), even a specially sized fire extinguisher ($8).

Engine options played a big role in determining a Mustang's personality. During the long 20-month 1965 model run, powerplant offerings were shuffled slightly. The original standard engine, the 101-bhp Falcon six, was dropped after September 1964 (considered the accepted

break between "1964½" and the "true" 1965 models). Its replacement was a 200-cid six with 120 bhp. The 200 was an improvement on the 170 because of its higher compression, redesigned valvetrain, and seven (instead of five) main bearings. It also featured an automatic choke, short-

stroke cylinder block for longer piston and cylinder wear, hydraulic valve lifters, and an intake manifold integral with the head.

The smallest V-8 initially offered was the modern 260-cid "thinwall" unit from the Fairlane, rated at 164 bhp. A bore enlarged from 3.80 to 4.00 inches made it a 289 (on the same 2.87-inch stroke), offering 195 bhp with two-barrel carburetor or 210 bhp with optional four-barrel carb (for $158 additional). A "Hi-Performance" (HP) four-barrel version delivered 271 bhp; price was $276 with the GT Group, $328 without. After September 1964, the 260

The 1964½ Mustang hardtop seen on these pages has the standard hubcaps. It is powered by the 260-cid, 164-bhp V-8, which boosted the sticker by $108. It also has Cruise-O-Matic ($179.80), console, radio, and more. The 260 V-8 was dropped in favor of the 289 after September 25, 1964.

was discontinued and a 200-bhp two-barrel 289 became the base V-8 option (at $106). Output of the standard four-barrel unit was then boosted to 225 bhp, while the "hi-po" version was unchanged.

These Ford small-blocks were classic V-8s—light, efficient, and powerful. Advanced thinwall casting techniques made them the lightest cast-iron V-8s on the market. Besides short-stroke design and hydraulic lifters, they featured full-length, full-circle water jackets; high turbulence, wedge-shaped combustion chambers; automatic choke; and centrifugal vacuum advance distributor.

The four-barrel engines achieved their extra power by increased carburetor air velocity matched to the engine's performance curve. They also had different valve timing compared with the two-barrel engines, plus a higher compression ratio that demanded premium fuel. The Hi-Performance 289 developed .95 bhp per cubic inch and offered 312 pounds-feet of torque at 3400 rpm. It featured a high-compression head, high-lift camshaft, free-breathing induction system, free-flow exhaust, solid lifters, low-restriction air cleaner, and chrome-plated valve stems.

Although the HP 289 seemed the answer to a dragster's dream, it could easily be tweaked for even more performance. A visit to your friendly Ford parts counter and about $500 would get you an impressive amount of "Cobra equipment." This included such items as special camshafts, heads, and intake manifolds; dual four-barrel carbs; and even Weber carbs. All these goodies were considered factory-stock, even though none were factory-installed. Said *Road & Track*: "The Cobra equipment will do a fabulous job if you set it up right, and you don't have to switch basic engines. You just bolt it onto your standard V-8. Also, this equipment will now be legal in the FX [National Hot Rod Association Factory Experimental] classes at the dragstrip."

Here's a rundown. Just $73 bought a Cobra cam kit consisting of solid lifters and a 306-degree-duration cam with 289-inch lift. The $222 cylinder head kit comprised two stock HP heads with extra-large intake and exhaust valves and heavy-duty valve springs and retainers. Matched pistons, combined with the cam and head kits, made up the $343 engine performance kit. Then there were carburetors and manifolds. A single four-barrel carb on a big-port aluminum manifold cost $120. Price with dual four-barrel was $243, with triple two-barrels $210. A final touch was

a dual-point centrifugal distributor, available at $50.

Even now, it's unclear exactly how much horsepower the Cobra bolt-ons could wring out of a Mustang engine. Ford's own dynamometer test of a stock HP 289 showed only 232 bhp at 5500 rpm, which was hardly the advertised 271 bhp at 6000 rpm. However, that was with all normal hardware installed; a stripped engine had been tested to get the advertised figure. A full-dress 289 with special distributor, hot heads, triple carbs, and special non-Cobra headers recorded 314 bhp at 6500 rpm, so 350 or more might not be too much to claim for a full-house Cobra-equipped engine. "You'll be able to feel that on the street," commented one engineer.

Ordering the Hi-Performance 289 meant you also had to take the extra-cost four-speed gearbox, which made the latter a "mandatory option," a contradiction in terms but an arrangement beloved in Sixties Detroit. The HP was also the only engine offered with the optional "short" rear axle ratios (3.89:1 and 4.11:1) so beloved by dragsters. Standard ratios were 3.20:1 with the six, 2.80 for the two-barrel V-8, 3.00 for the four-barrel V-8, and 3.50 with the HP. It could be argued that ratios like

This page: The styled steel wheels (*top*) sported the Mustang logo. This car features Rally-Pac instruments and a four-speed manual. *Opposite page*: Lee Iacocca orchestrated the debut of the Mustang well, for only six weeks after it bowed at the New York World's Fair it served as the Indy 500 Pace Car (*top*). In its short model year, the 1964 ½ Mustang saw 28,833 ragtops built.

2.80:1 made the milder Mustangs over-geared, but this appealed to customers who preferred economy and quiet highway cruising over lightning-quick getaway.

Front disc brakes were offered beginning late in the '65 model year and were well worth the money. Built by Kelsey-Hayes, they were one-piece cast-iron units with a disc diameter of 9.5 inches. A radial rib separated the two braking surfaces, and each pad was actuated by two cylinders. Discs were a valuable option because the Mustang's ordinary front drums were noted for neither stopping power nor fade resistance.

Arriving with the rest of the '65 Ford line in autumn 1964 was a snazzy Mustang coupe with semi-fastback styling, a late-in-the-game idea prompted partly by the surprising, renewed buyer interest in "torpedo" shapes (though they were nothing like their Forties forebears). Several names were considered, including GT Limited, Grand Sport and, tellingly, GTO, but the final nameplates read "2+2." That was apt, because rear legroom was scanty —even less than in the hardtop or convertible. But there was compensation in an optional fold-down rear seat, with a partition in the trunk bulkhead that also

dropped forward to create a long load platform that could accommodate items like skis or fishing rods. Instead of rear quarter windows, the 2+2 had gill-like C-pillar air vents, part of its flow-through ventilation system.

This page: Wire-wheel covers were a popular option on '65 Mustangs; they cost $45.80 and could be had only with 14-inch wheels, which were standard with the V-8. *Opposite*: The trunk rack was not seen often, but was a stylish—and practical—extra.

The semi-fastback bowed on October 1, 1964, wearing 2+2 badging (*top*). The 200-cid six (*above*) was made standard at the same time; it cranked out 120 horsepower, enough to give the 2589-pound 2+2 fairly peppy performance. The 2+2 (*right*) sported air extractors on the rear pillars in place of a rear side window.

Sales of the Mustang 2+2 got off to a good start: 77,079 were built for the 1965 model year. A base price of $2589 didn't hurt a bit, although well-equipped models sold for up to $4000. The GT package was popular; it put together some bits and pieces aimed at pleasing the enthusiast. The option was highlighted with a modest red badge on the front fenders (*opposite*); the side stripes were a delete option. The 289 V-8 (*right*) was the workhorse that powered most 1965 Mustangs. It came in horsepower ratings of 200 with a two-barrel carb, 225 with four-barrel, and 271 bhp in an all-out version that ran on 10.5:1 compression and swilled prodigious amounts of premium gas.

Mustang's long-hood/short-deck proportions quickly set the pattern for what came to be known, in its honor, as the "ponycar"; in other words, a low-priced personal sportster of similar shape. Competitors reacted to the new theme, as quickly as they could but it took time. It wasn't until 1967 that Chevrolet and Pontiac brought out the Camaro and Firebird. Ford's sister division, Lincoln-Mercury, also needed two years to ready its Mustang-based Cougar. On the other hand, tiny American Motors moved fairly rapidly in getting out its shapely Javelin for '68. Chrysler's entry was the Plymouth Barracuda, a "glassback" derivative of the compact Valiant introduced within weeks of the Mustang. The timing was mere

coincidence, but many nevertheless viewed Barracuda as a Mustang reply, though it really wasn't. It didn't have the same kind of style until it was handsomely overhauled, also for '67. Mustang thus had the ponycar field all to itself for a minimum of two years, giving Ford Division that much of a head start on rivals.

Though undeniably attractive, the Mustang was not an exotic or earthshaking piece of design; its generally clean lines still showed traces of gingerbread. For example,

Although the '66 Mustang (*this page*) didn't differ greatly from the '65 (*opposite*), there were a number of detail changes. Note, for example, the revised standard hubcaps (*top row*) and how the grille and the fake side vents were altered (*bottom row*).

the bright "scoops" ahead of the rear wheel openings weren't functional; the shallow, high-set grille looked awkward; and detail execution around the headlights and at the rear wasn't faultless.

Space utilization, given the 108-inch wheelbase, wasn't so hot, either. A Mustang really wasn't habitable for four adults on a long trip, and trunk space was as meager as rear legroom. Limited passenger space was characteristic of all ponycars, the price of their racy proportions. This may partly explain why ponycar popularity declined rapidly in the early Seventies as buyers became more attuned to space-efficient engineering from Europe and Japan.

Enthusiast magazines had other criticisms. *Road & Track*, in particular, wasn't happy with the driving position, citing a deep-dish steering wheel set too close to the driver's chest, too little leg space between the clutch and the nearest interfering object (the turn indicator lever), sparse standard instrumentation, and bucket seats only marginally effective in holding occupants in place. The Mustang's low list price, *R&T* decided, was responsible for such lapses. But the editors admitted that the car was carpeted, trimmed, and finished "in a manner that many European sports/touring cars would do well to emulate."

With standard suspension, a Mustang was anything but a grand tourer in the European mold. "The ride is wallowy, there's a tendency for the car to float when being driven at touring speeds, and the 'porpoise' factor is high on an undulating surface," *R&T* noted. "There's just nothing

different about it in this respect....There seems little excuse for such frankly sloppy suspension on any car with the sporting characteristics which have been claimed for the Mustang."

As for straight-line performance, *R&T*'s 210-bhp/four-speed car did about what the editors expected: 0-60 mph in nine seconds; the standing quarter-mile in 16.5 seconds at 80 mph; top speed of 110 mph. Fuel consumption was 14-18 mpg. *R&T* applauded Mustang's good looks and low price, but regretted that it was otherwise little different from "the typical American sedan."

The "Pony" interior (*above*)—with Mustangs stampeding across the seatbacks—is much coveted by collectors today. In addition to the Rally-Pac gauges, this interior (*below left*) is notable for the factory air conditioning (only 9.6 percent of the '66s had it) and the lack of a console. With air, underhood plumbing became a bit more complicated (*below*). *Opposite page*: Mustangs ordered with the GT package got their own gas cap. Mustang production totaled 607,568 units for 1966, good for a 7.1 percent market share and enough to make Mustang the third best-selling nameplate in the industry.

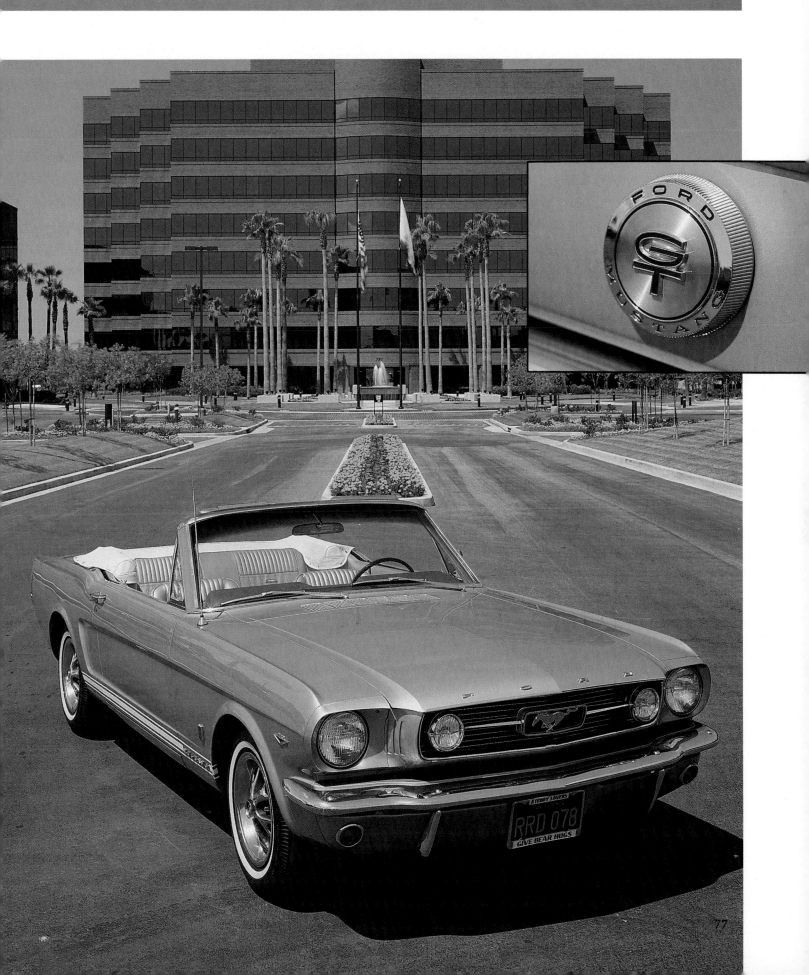

Then the magazine laid hands on a properly optioned Mustang, and its opinion changed radically. With the 271-bhp Hi-Performance V-8, this second *R&T* tester impressed with much improved performance. Its 0-60-mph time, for example, was a more exciting 8.3 seconds.

But the editors were even more impressed with the changes wrought by the optional and inexpensive handling package. This consisted of stiff springs and shocks, a larger-diameter front anti-sway bar, 5.90 × 15 Firestone Super Sports tires, and a quicker steering ratio (3.5 turns lock-to-lock). "The effect is to eliminate the wallow we experienced with previous Mustangs, and to tie the car to the road much more firmly, so on a fast run the point of one's departure into the boondocks is delayed very considerably," *R&T* wrote. "There is a certain harshness to the ride at low speeds over poor surfaces, but this is a small price to pay for the great improvement in handling and roadholding." There was a marked degree of oversteer present in this car, even though 56 percent of its weight was on the front wheels, but its

hard suspension, *R&T* said, inspired more driver confidence.

R&T cheered the HP Mustang as "a big step in the right direction," but looked forward to disc brakes and independent rear suspension. Until then, the editors said they'd be "reluctantly unconquered." The discs showed up as an option within months, but irs never materialized.

As a voice for what Iacocca called "the sports car crowd, the real buffs," *Road & Track* was among the harshest of the enthusiast publications in its judgment of the Mustang. By contrast, *Motor Trend*, a magazine whose tastes have traditionally favored Detroit products, liked all versions of the car, the HP in particular. *MT* scored 7.6 seconds in the 0-60-mph sprint and

Opposite page: Among the many options available to Mustang buyers were a vinyl roof and pin striping around the side scallop (*top*) in lieu of the standard simulated side vents. Many buyers preferred the $58.24 wire-wheel hubcaps (*bottom*) over the $93.84 styled steel wheels. *This page*: The 2+2 listed at $2607 in 1966, just $46 less than a ragtop.

ran the quarter-mile in slightly less time than *Road & Track*. It was obvious that, with the right options, Mustang could be quite an automobile indeed.

The HP Mustang received an even more glowing endorsement from no less an expert than race driver Dan Gurney. Writing in *Popular Science*, he stated: "This car will run the rubber off a Triumph or MG. It has the feel of a 2+2 Ferrari. So what *is* a sports car?" Gurney's mount did 123 mph maximum and consistently beat a similarly equipped Corvette in quarter-mile acceleration runs. If Ford hadn't created a true sports car in the HP Mustang, it had certainly come close.

Mustang seemed born to race, and did even before it went on sale. In late winter of 1963-64, Ford prepped a team of rally Mustangs to take over for the newly banned Falcon Sprints in European events,

but their only major win came in the Tour de France, where Peter Proctor and Peter Harper finished one-two in class.

There was more success on the dragstrips, where 2+2s stuffed full of Ford's 427-cid big-block racked up numerous wins in NHRA's A/FX class and, less often, as "funny cars." The factory got into the act for the '65 season, fielding wild "altereds" on two-inch-shorter wheelbases. At the Pomona Winternationals in February, Bill Lawton's Mustang outlasted and outpaced a pack of Comets, Mustangs, and Mopars to win A/FX. Les Ritchey did the same at the Labor Day Nationals in Indianapolis, beating famed dragster Gas Rhonda.

With Mustang sales roaring along as the 1966 model year approached, Ford product planners saw little reason to tamper with success, though new or mostly new Detroit designs rarely see major

The '66 Mustang convertible weighed in at 2650 pounds, and sold for $2653. That was just the beginning, however. The two-barrel Challenger 289 added $105.63 to the tab, the four-barrel $158.48. Air conditioning, as on this car (*above*), upped the ante another $310.90. Other options seen here: radio and antenna, $57.51; power brakes, $42.29; Cruise-O-Matic, $185.39; deluxe wood-grain steering wheel, $31.52; MagicAire heater, $45.45 (delete option).

changes in their sophomore season. But though the '66 looked like a '65 rerun at first glance, there were changes.

Up front, the honeycomb grille texture was replaced by thin bars, and the thick horizontal chrome bar was discarded, leaving the galloping horse to float in its chromed rectangular frame. Mustang GTs kept the grille bar, however, with auxiliary driving lights mounted at its ends. At the rear was a restyled fuel filler cap. Along the sides, the simulated rear wheel scoop was decorated with three windsplits (except on GTs, 2+2s, and luxury models, which didn't have this trim); front fender name-plates and emblems were revised; and GTs got an additional plaque. Finally, the stock wheel covers were redesigned.

Inside alterations were more functional. For example, the original Falcon-style instrument cluster with its old-fashioned strip speedometer was replaced by the

five-gauge unit with round speedo previously reserved for the GT package. The Rally-Pac tachometer/clock combination, mounted on the steering column, was still an option.

Running-gear changes included upgrading six-cylinder models from 13- to 14-inch wheels and reworking engine mounts for all models to reduce vibration. Engine choices remained at four: standard 200-cid six and the three optional 289s.

The option list was extended to include a stereo cartridge tape player ($128) and deluxe seatbelts with remainder warning light ($15).

Predictably, Mustang's 1966 sales were down compared with model year '65, which was longer than usual due to the early introduction. But for comparable 12-month periods, the '66s actually ran ahead by 50,000 units. Mustang still had no direct competition and romped along

Mustang's base engine for 1966, a 200-cubic-inch six (*far left*), was rated at 120 horsepower at 4400 rpm. It featured hydraulic valve lifters, seven main bearings, a one-barrel Autolite carburetor, and a 9.2:1 compression ratio. With 499,751 built, the hardtop was easily the most popular body style, seen here as a Sprint 200 (*opposite, center*). The convertible (*bottom and below*) tallied up 35,698 orders, way down from the 1965 total.

at close to half a million hardtops, 70,000 convertibles, and 35,000 fastbacks.

Ford promoted the six-cylinder Mustang quite vigorously for '66. "We felt there was a need to emphasize the economy aspect at that time," one Ford executive remembers. "Also, the six-cylinder coupe was by then the only Mustang selling for less than Mr. Iacocca's original target figure." (It listed at $2416, attractive indeed.)

Though it looked like its V-8 counterpart, the six-cylinder Mustang was considerably different under the skin. Its wheels had only four lugs, while V-8 wheels had five. All Mustangs had standard drum brakes, but sixes had nine-inchers, V-8s 10-inchers. The six-cylinder cars also had a lighter rear axle and a slightly narrower front track, and their spring rates were somewhat lower to keep an even keel; they would have looked tail-heavy had they used the heavier V-8 suspension.

The standard drum brakes, though, were quite effective with the six, capable of slightly shorter stopping distances from 60 mph than a V-8 car's discs, though they were susceptible to fade on repeated hard applications. The Mustang six performed reasonably well for a car of its class. *Motor Trend*'s automatic-equipped model ran 0-60 mph in 14.3 seconds and averaged 20 mpg on regular gas.

Some criticisms in Mustang road tests of the period concerned minor irritations such as the lack of rear-seat ashtrays and armrests or the absence of dashboard-level interior lights. But the one consistent gripe remained lack of interior room. "Five passengers can fit," wrote *Motor Trend*, "but the fifth one usually sits on the other four's nerves." However, *MT* summed up the Mustang as "safe and roadworthy, easy to handle, and fun to drive" in spite of its size limitations.

By this time, Ford was aware that competitors were readying ponycars of their own, but this had little to do with the more substantial changes that were already in the works for the '67 Mustang. These were initiated in mid-1964, just as the country was catching "Mustang fever," and reflected both the industry's usual three-year lead time and, to some extent, Ford's uncertainty at that point on how the original concept would "play in Peoria." Of course, once the orders started pouring in, Ford realized that it didn't have to alter the basic car *that* much.

1965-66 MUSTANG AT A GLANCE

Model Year Production

No.	Model	1965*	1966
63A	Fastback, standard	71,303	27,809
63B	Fastback, deluxe	5,776	7,889
65A	Hardtop, standard	464,828	422,416
65B	Hardtop, deluxe	22,232	55,938
65C	Hardtop, bench seat	14,905	21,397
76A	Convertible, standard	94,496	56,409
76B	Convertible, deluxe	5,338	12,520
76C	Convertible, bench seat	2,111	3,190
	TOTAL	680,989	607,568

*April 1964-August 1965

Prices/Weights
($/lbs)

07	Hardtop, I-6	$2372/2445	$2416/2488
07	Hardtop, V-8	2480/2720	—
08	Convertible, I-6	2614/2669	2653/2650
08	Convertible, V-8	2722/2904	—
09	Fastback, I-6	2589/2495	2607/2519
09	Fastback, V-8	2697/2770	—

General Specifications

	1964½	1965	1966
Wheelbase (in.)	108.0	108.0	108.0
Overall length (in.)	181.6	181.6	181.6
Overall width (in.)	68.2	68.2	68.2
Std. Trans.	3-sp. man.	3-sp. man.	3-sp.man.
Optional Trans.	overdrive 4-sp. man. 3-sp. auto	overdrive 4-sp. man. 3-sp. auto	overdrive 4-sp. man. 3-sp. auto

Engine Availability

Type	cid	bhp	1964½	1965	1966
I-6	170	101	Std.	—	—
I-6	200	120	—	Std.	Std.
V-8	260	164	Std.	—	—
V-8	289	200	Opt.	Std.	Opt.
V-8	289	225	Opt.	Opt.	Opt.
V-8	289	271	Opt.	Opt.	Opt.

Nevertheless, the annual model change was a fact of life in the go-go Sixties, and change for its own sake was mostly behind the first major step in Mustang's evolution. The result was a bolder and brawnier 1967 model that started Ford's lithe and lovely ponycar down the path of bigger-is-better, a seven-year journey that would ultimately lead back to square one.

The GT equipment group, as seen on this '66 soft top (*opposite*), listed at $152.20. It required a V-8 and included dual exhausts, grille-mounted fog lamps, disc brakes, handling package, and GT racing stripes on the sides. The luggage rack sold for a modest $32.44. A group of competitors would invade Mustang territory in 1967, leaving 1966 as the historic high water mark in Mustang popularity.

CHAPTER FOUR

1967-68:
More
and Less

9-16-65
S-9127-2

9-16-65
S-9127-4

It takes time to get a car to market, anywhere from three to five years, depending on the company. This means that stylists and engineers must often begin work on the next phase of a design before they know how the public liked the one they just finished—a curious shot-in-the-dark approach that's nonetheless traditional in this industry (and a few others, too).

The '67 Mustang was no exception. Ford commenced initial studies for it in the early summer of 1964, just as the first Mustang was catching fire all across the country. Yet the very fact of Mustang's phenomenal early success raised some vexing questions. With the original design scheduled to run through 1966, Ford planners knew that the '67s would need more substantial changes. But how extensive should those be? As the months rolled by and sales soared, it was realized that changing the car too much might put a damper on demand.

Then again, Ford wasn't sure in mid-1964 that the ponycar craze wasn't just a flash in the pan. True, it wasn't long before we started hearing of "Mustangers" and the "Mustang Generation" (and a whole slew of merchandising tie-ins for these youthful buyers). But as product planner Ross Humphries later told author Gary Witzenburg: "At the time the '67 was planned, we really didn't have any idea

that the original was such a winner. Things did look awfully rosy, but we didn't know how long it was going to last." So what Ford had to decide was, should the '67 be simply more of the same or more obviously different; and if different, how?

There was also the question of when the competition might respond, and how. Plymouth had launched its Valiant-based Barracuda fastback at about the same time as Mustang, but it was far less distinctive

and no real sales threat. Arch-rival Chevrolet was another matter. For a time, General Motors design chief William L. Mitchell insisted that his company had a Mustang-fighter in the beautiful second-generation Corvair of 1965, but this was only a smokescreen for the super-secret Camaro, a true Chevy ponycar being rushed out for '67. As Ford engineer Tom Feaheny later admitted: "It was a long ways down the road before we were aware

Opposite page: The styling of the 1967 Mustang had been pretty well locked in by September 1965. Ford knew that Chevy was busy working on its own "ponycar" for 1967, so the '67 Mustang received more extensive changes than it would have gotten otherwise. The '67 Mustang (*above*) still rode a 108-inch wheelbase. This one has the springtime Sprint option that included directional indicators in the hood.

that they were coming after us. The party line at GM was that the Corvair *was* their answer to the Mustang, and we were kind of believing it."

Beyond this, a good many Ford engineers, stung by press criticism of the original Mustang, were just itching to attend to details. "[The '67] was an opportunity to do a lot of refinement work," said Feaheny. "Frankly, the amount of engineering in that [first Mustang] was not as great as it could have been. It did not get the full-blown effort it really deserved....We really wanted to do the job right the second time around." Feaheny also pointed to the influence of Ford Division product planning chief Hal Sperlich. "[His] philosophy on the '67 Mustang was to one-up the original in every respect: model availability, options, handling, performance, braking, comfort,

quietness, even appearance where we could without making a major change."

Last but not least was the need to "commonize" Mustang front-end componentry with that of the new-for-'66 Fairlane and Falcon (specifically, relocating the coil springs above the upper front

crossmembers) for reasons of cost-savings and assembly-line efficiency. And since Pontiac's pioneer muscle car, the GTO, had also arrived to great acclaim in mid-1964, Ford decided it might as well take the opportunity to enlarge the Mustang engine bay to accept big-block V-8 power,

As before, the '67 Mustang could be equipped with the GT Equipment Group. The "A" behind the GT on the car seen above indicates that it has an automatic transmission mated to its 390 V-8. The '67 was a bit bigger in every direction and weight was up on the base model by about 80 pounds.

correctly concluding that even a ponycar could always use more performance to keep pace with a burgeoning new horsepower race.

All this resulted in a '67 Mustang that retained its predecessor's basic chassis, inner structure, and running gear but was new most everywhere else. The big change, of course, was the planned big-block V-8: the familiar 390-cubic-inch "Thunderbird Special" unit with four-barrel carburetor and a rousing 320 bhp, standard on that year's Thunderbird and available for big Fords and the intermediate Fairlane. As a Mustang option it cost $264, versus $434 for the "hi-po" small-block. Dealers usually recommended that it be teamed with Ford's new "SelectShift" Cruise-O-Matic transmission, which cost $233 with either of

the top-power V-8s. SelectShift referred to a special "manual" feature that allowed this automatic to be held in its two lower gears for maximum acceleration. The 390, which came with heavy-duty three-speed manual, brought the number of Mustang powerteams to 13.

Though it certainly made for potent performance, the 390 also made for a very

Mustang received a new dashboard for 1967 (*top row*). The two big dials housed the speedometer and optional tachometer. The fastback was a true fastback for '67; the ribbed rear panel (*center right*) was optional. The triple taillights were now fully separated and the grille opening was both larger and lower.

front-heavy Mustang (fully 58 percent of total curb weight) that understeered with merry abandon. The option included F70-14 Firestone Wide-Oval tires that helped reduce this somewhat, but almost anyone who drove a 390 said that a 289 Mustang handled far better.

Customers were also well-advised to order the 390 with the optional $389 Competition Handling Package, though this meant you also had to order the GT Group. Also available with the HP small-block, it comprised stiffer springs and front stabilizer bar, Koni adjustable shocks, limited-slip differential with 3.25:1 final drive, quick-ratio steering, and 15-inch wheels, all of which improved handling at the expense of ride. Predictably perhaps, few buyers bothered with the Competition option, making it quite rare today.

Of course, the payoff for big-block buyers was spectacular acceleration.

Typical figures were 0-60 mph in 7.5 seconds, the standing quarter-mile in 15.5 seconds at 95 mph, and a top speed of close to 120 mph. If not the fastest Detroiter of 1967, the 390 Mustang was certainly right in there with the top five percent of production automobiles.

Matching this burly new engine option was a more muscular look from the beltline down via new outer sheetmetal that preserved all the familiar Mustang "cues" in softer, shapelier styling. The 2+2 got a sweeping full-fastback roofline partly inspired by that of Ford's GT40 endurance racer, though the earlier, slightly notched effect was in contention for a time. So were straight-through beltlines; crisp, "formal" contours like those of Mercury's new Mustang-based luxury ponycar, the '67 Cougar; elliptical side window openings; and various exaggerated scoops, scallops, and sculptures.

But all of this was swept aside for a "more Mustang" look. This mainly involved a concave tail panel, a noticeable rear-fender kick-up aft of the doors, and a few extra inches in the nose to match a more aggressive grille bereft of flanking gill-like impressions. And, oh yes: The single three-element taillamps were now separate units. A new Exterior Decor Group put thin bars on the back panel and turn-signal repeater lights in a special twin-scoop hood. Combining the GT option with automatic got you "GT/A" badges on the lower front fenders. Wheelbase was unchanged, but overall length went up by two inches, width by 2.7 inches and front track 2.6 inches.

That last change was significant. It was made largely to provide adequate room for the bulky big-block V-8, but it also benefited handling. As mentioned, front springs were relocated above the top

The '67 Mustang looked more aggressive than the 1965-66 series because of its more forward-thrusting grille and longer snout. The convertible started at $2698; the styled steel wheels cost an extra $115, the trunk-mounted luggage rack $32. Although total Mustang sales were down in 1967, convertible deliveries increased by about 20 percent to 44,808.

crossmember, as in the Fairlane. At the same time, the upper A-arm pivot was lowered and the roll center raised, a change picked up from Carroll Shelby's GT-350 (see Chapter 11). The effect was to decrease understeer by holding the outside front wheel exactly perpendicular to the road. Since this didn't require higher spring rates, ride didn't suffer. Engineers also paid attention to reducing noise, vibration, and harshness (NVH) with new rubber bushings at suspension attachment points.

The '67 shed another vestige of Mustang's Falcon origins with an imposing new "twin-cowl" instrument panel, dominated by a pair of large, circular dials ahead of the driver, surmounted by three smaller gauges. Ordering the optional tachometer eliminated the ammeter and oil pressure gauges in the starboard slot, a retrograde step, but the bulkier dash made room for integrating the air conditioner. (The previous hang-on unit was still available as a dealer accessory.) Newly optional for all

models was the useful Tilt-Away steering wheel from the Thunderbird, as well as a "Convenience Control Panel," a set of four warning lights mounted above the radio top and center.

Against its new rivals, the '67 Mustang compared quite favorably. With the economical six, it was more miserly than a like-equipped Barracuda or Camaro yet still had decent performance because the Mustang was generally lighter. Ford also offered a wider selection of V-8s than its competitors, though the Camaro's optional 375-bhp 396 had the edge on any other ponycar in straight-line performance. Mustang was less roomy and had a smaller

The Mustang didn't change much outwardly for 1968. Most noticeable was a slightly altered grille that featured a chrome surround just inside the grille cavity and new—and still fake—air vents ahead of the rear wheels. Prices for 1968 were $2602 for the six-cylinder hardtop, $2712 for the fastback 2+2, and $2814 for the convertible.

trunk than the Barracuda, though the fastback versions of both had a fold-down back seat and trunk partition. The Mustang rode a bit harder than the Camaro and was noisier than either Camaro or Barracuda. On the other hand, it had a new option the others didn't: the swing-away steering wheel straight from the T-Bird. Also, the '67 convertible top gained a rear window of articulated glass, which was superior to plastic. (A horizontal crease allowed it to "bend" as the top folded down.) With the handsome new '67 Barracuda, all three cars were nice-looking, so buyer preference was largely a matter of individual taste.

New competition—including some intramural interference from corporate cousin Cougar—naturally hurt Mustang in 1967 model year sales: down approximately 25 percent from '66. The top-selling hardtop sustained much of this loss. The convertible and fastback exchanged places in popularity, the former dropping to only about 45,000 units, the latter moving up to over 70,000 by virtue of its slick new styling. But 472,121 sales was hardly bad for any car in 1967, and the ponycar originator remained the ponycar pacesetter by a wide margin—more than 2 to 1 over Camaro, its closest challenger. Interestingly, '67 Mustang sales were more than *double* the most optimistic estimates of Ford's

marketing mavens for the model's *first* year.

As if to answer the question of some Ford planners—Why change a good thing?—Mustang sales plummeted for 1968. On paper the losses were difficult to explain. It was a year of improving sales for the industry in general and Ford Division in particular, and Mustang offered the widest selection of engines and convenience options in its brief history. The likely answer was continued competition,

now rougher than ever. Besides GM and Chrysler, American Motors was a threat with its new Javelin and AMX. Also, Mustang prices were higher than before. The convertible's base list was up over $2800, for example, and a handful of options could run that to over $4000, which was quite a sum in those days.

Competition from other Ford Division products was also a factor. The Mustang fastback, with sales plunging to about

40,000, had a major rival in the Ford Torino, the new top-line series in the intermediate Fairlane line and the 1968 replacement for the Fairlane 500XL and GT as Ford's muscle car. Besides a notchback hardtop and a convertible, the lineup included a slick new fastback in Torino GT and Fairlane 500 trim. It was visibly larger than the Mustang (201 inches long overall, versus 184), and it had a genuine rear seat because of its 116-inch wheelbase (eight inches longer than Mustang's). The mid-size fastback's sleek lines were quite similar to the slope-roof Mustang's, as were those of rivals like the Barracuda and Dodge's new "fuselage-style" mid-size Charger. The Torino GT version accounted for over 74,000 sales in its debut season, and it's reasonable to suggest that a healthy portion of those would have otherwise been Mustang fastbacks.

Familiarity may have been another factor in Mustang's '68 sales slide, particularly as styling was little changed after 1967's major facelift. As before, the trademark simulated air scoops ahead of the rear wheels were integrated with the side sculpture via a crease line running from the upper front fender to behind and around the scoop, then down and forward into the lower part of the door. GTs now accented this with optional "C-stripes" that imparted a look of motion. All '68s carried a more deeply inset grille, the galloping horse still in a bright rectangle that was newly flush-mounted (rather than ahead of the insert). Eliminating the horizontal grille bar left GT foglamps to "float" at the outboard ends of the big mouth cavity.

The rest of the GT package was essentially unchanged. The '68 edition also included dual exhausts with chrome-plated "quad" outlets, a pop-open fuel filler cap, heavy-duty suspension (high-rate springs plus HD shocks and front sway bar), F70-14 whitewall tires on six-inch rims, and styled steel wheels. Wide-Oval tires were also available.

Much to the delight of enthusiasts, Mustang continued with the GT package for 1968. It cost $147, to which had to be added $264 for the 390 V-8 (*left*), which cranked out a thumping 325 horsepower. Unfortunately, it also made the Mustang a bit nose heavy. Ford built 42,325 Mustang fastbacks for 1968.

Mustang engine offerings were more numerous than ever for '68, but some had to be detuned to meet the new federal emission standards that now applied to all 50 states. Compression eased from 9.2:1 to 8.8:1 left the 200-cid six at 115 bhp, down five, while a similar cut lowered the two-barrel 289 V-8 to 195 bhp, versus the previous 200. However, rated horsepower on the big 390 actually *increased*, to 335. And for the first time, there was an optional six: a 250-cid unit lifted from Ford's truck line, offering 155 bhp for just $26. Four-speed manual was no longer available for six-cylinder Mustangs.

Sadly, the high-winding four-barrel 289 was dropped as the middle V-8. Taking its place was a considerably changed small-block stroked out to 302 cid (bore and stroke: 4.00 × 3.00 inches) for a rated 230

bhp. A tractable, reasonably economical compromise, it cost only about $200.

Topping the chart at a whopping $755 was the mighty 427-cid enlargement of the Ford big-block, with 10.9:1 compression and a conservative 390-bhp rating. Though restricted to Cruise-O-Matic, it was good for 0-60-mph times in the neighborhood of six seconds, making for the fastest showroom-stock Mustang yet. But its heaviness (which tended to overwhelm the front suspension) and that

One of the more interesting Mustangs offered in 1968 was the GT/CS (*opposite page*). The "CS" stood for California Special, but it might just as well have stood for Carroll Shelby since the CS was a limited edition model that borrowed much of its looks from the mean Shelby GT-350/500s. Features included unique side striping and side air vents, rear spoiler, and Shelby-style taillights. The regular convertible (*below*) could look pretty mean, too.

formidable price precluded many sales.

Then again, the 427 was intended for serious drivers only. This was an enormously powerful engine for a light car like Mustang, and though its blistering acceleration was attractive, it could also induce very pronounced oversteer, a handling trait not all that familiar to the average motorist.

For most buyers, the 390 was much more flexible and practical. It could be teamed with three- or four-speed manual transmission as well as automatic, and could yield over 15 mpg in conservative driving. It was tractable in traffic, idled smoothly, and was mild-mannered at low speeds. Although it added extra weight to the front end compared with the six or small-block V-8s, this wasn't usually noticeable unless you poked your foot to the floor.

Incidentally, big-block-powered '68

Mustangs benefited from the addition of floating calipers to the power front-disc-brake option. These provided more stopping force than the fixed-caliper '67 discs with the same amount of pedal effort. The new design was also said to promote longer brake life and, with fewer parts, to be more reliable. Ford recognized the need for front discs in big-engine Mustangs by making them a mandatory option for all cars equipped with the 390 or 427.

The 427 was hastily retired at mid-year. In its place came the 428 Cobra Jet, a huskier version of the big-block lately

The **California Special** featured a plain grille cavity set off with foglamps and *no* Mustang emblem. Hood locks can also be seen on this example. Most CS models were in fact sold in the Golden State, their mission being to give flagging Mustang sales a shot in the arm.

familiar in the Thunderbird and big Fords. For drag racing and insurance purposes, it was advertised at 335 bhp on 10.7:1 compression, but was undoubtedly much stronger. A quarter-mile zip of 13.56 seconds at a trap speed of 106.64 mph caused *Hot Rod* magazine to sing its praises.

Announced at about the same time was a fortified 302 with high-compression heads, larger valves, wilder cam timing, and a pair of four-barrel carbs. Humorously rated at 240 bhp, it was clearly developed for Trans-Am racing, but Ford had trouble getting it into production after getting SCCA's okay, and few were actually made. It didn't matter: Mark Donohue's Camaro won 10 events to Mustang's three, and Chevy collected the manufacturers' trophy.

New to Mustang's lengthening options list was the Sports Trim Group, with

woodgrain dash, two-tone hood paint (also available separately), Comfort-Weave vinyl seat inserts, and wheel lip moldings on sixes, plus styled-steel wheels and larger tires with V-8. Other new extras included rear-window defogger and Fingertip Speed Control. A spring/summer Sprint package offered GT C-stripes, pop-open gas cap, and full wheel covers plus, with V-8, styled wheels and Wide-Oval tires.

Despite all the go-go goodies, installation rates suggested buyers were shifting from pure sport to a combination of sport and luxury. Cruise-O-Matic, for example, was

No matter if it was a California Special—all 1968 Mustangs had to meet new federal standards, including one that called for side marker lights front and rear. CS models are avidly sought by collectors nowadays.

fitted to 72 percent of '68 production (four-speeds amounted to a mere six percent), power steering to 52 percent of the cars, and air conditioning to 18 percent. Power front-disc-brake installations were only 13 percent, though they'd rise to 31 percent the following year.

Appearing only during the '68 season was a somewhat rare, limited-production Mustang, the California Special. Offered primarily in the Golden State and styled along the lines of the Shelby-Mustang GTs, it was basically the standard hardtop with a ducktail spoiler above wide Cougar-like taillight clusters, plus mid-bodyside tape stripes and a plain grille cavity with foglamps but no Mustang emblem.

As elsewhere in Detroit, Mustang boasted several new safety features for '68, some added at Ford's discretion but most required by the government. These comprised energy-absorbing instrument panel and steering column, retractable seatbelts front and rear, standard backup lights, dual-circuit brake system, hazard warning flashers, side marker lights, energy-absorbing seatbacks, front seatback catches, positive door-lock buttons, safety door handles, double-yoke door latches, padded sunvisors and windshield pillars, double-thick laminated windshield, day/night rearview mirror on a breakaway mount, outside rearview mirror, safety-rim wheels, and load-rated tires. Also included were corrosion-resistant brake lines and a standardized shift quadrant with automatic transmission. To meet government specs for glare, Ford put a dull finish on windshield wiper arms, steering wheel hub and horn ring, rearview mirror, and windshield pillars.

Among Ford-designed features continued from previous Mustangs were reversible keys and 6000-mile lube- and oil-change intervals. Another popular item was the 5/50-24/24 warranty. This covered powertrain, suspension, steering, and wheels for five years or 50,000 miles, whichever came first; other components were warranted for 24 months or 24,000 miles. A second owner could assume any unused portion of the guarantee for a fee not exceeding $25.

At over 300,000 units for 1968, Mustang sales were good, though not great. But this was far below the heady days of 1965-66, when Iacocca's brainchild had earned over a million sales. Though no one knew it at the time, it was a sign that the ponycar market was nearing its peak barely four years after Mustang started the stampede.

No matter. Ford was about to take a new direction with its ponycar. With the still bolder and brasher '69, Mustang would never be the same again.

1967-68 MUSTANG AT A GLANCE

Model Year Production

No.	Model	1967	1968
63A	Fastback, standard	53,651	33,585
63B	Fastback, deluxe	17,391	7,661
63C	Fastback, bench seat	—	1,079
63D	Fastback, deluxe bench seat	—	256
65A	Hardtop, standard	325,853	233,472
65B	Hardtop, deluxe	22,228	9,009
65C	Hardtop, bench seat	8,190	6,113
65D	Hardtop, deluxe bench seat	—	853
76A	Convertible, standard	38,751	22,037
76B	Convertible, deluxe	4,848	3,339
76C	Convertible, bench seat	1,209	—
	TOTAL	472,121	317,404

Prices/Weights
($/lbs)

	Models	1967	1968
01	Hardtop, I-6	$2461/2568	$2602/2635
03	Convertible, I-6	$2698/2738	$2814/2745
02	Fastback, I-6	$2592/2605	$2712/2659

General Specifications

	1967	1968
Wheelbase (in.)	108.0	108.0
Overall length (in.)	183.6	183.6
Overall width (in.)	70.9	70.9
Std. Trans.	3-sp. man.	3-sp. man.
Optional Trans.	4-sp. man. 3-sp. auto.	4-sp. man. 3-sp. auto.

Engine Availability

Type	cid	bhp	1967	1968
I-6	200	120	Std.	—
I-6	200	115	—	Std.
V-8	289	195/200	Opt.	Opt.
V-8	289	225	Opt.	—
V-8	289	271	Opt.	—
V-8	302	230	—	Opt.
V-8	390	320/325	Opt.	Opt.
V-8	427	390	—	Opt.

The Mach 1 show car was clearly based on the Mustang, but was much lower and sported a number of unique features, such as the functional air scoops on the sides, "toll booth" side windows, racing-style fuel filler caps, and quadruple exhausts. It was a forerunner of the 1968 Mach I show car and the production Mustang Mach I that would debut in 1969.

CHAPTER FIVE

1969-70:
Horses
for
Courses

The 1969 Mustang was unveiled about four months after General Motors veteran Semon E. "Bunkie" Knudsen was named Ford Motor Company president in February 1968. It did not, therefore, reflect his influence. Records show the basic '69 design was more or less finished a year before Knudsen moved in.

Nevertheless, Ford vigorously emphasized racy styling and high performance under Knudsen, and the '69 Mustang coincidentally reflected this by offering something for everyone. No longer content with just a sporty personal car that could be tailored to taste, Ford now took the Mustang into the worlds of grand touring,

luxury, and ultra-high performance with the Mach 1, Grandé, and Boss models. Though all '69s retained the basic body package and 108-inch wheelbase from previous years, they were changed in almost every other dimension. They were also somewhat more roadable than their predecessors, and some were very quick.

The Cobra Jet Mach 1 and Boss 302 would be the fastest production Mustangs save the Shelby GTs (see Chapter 11)—Ford's responses to the challenges of the Camaro Z-28 and Firebird Trans Am.

Detroit gasped in astonishment when Knudsen resigned as GM executive vice-president to answer Henry Ford II's invitation. There probably hadn't been such a startling executive shift since Bunkie's father, William S. Knudsen, had left Ford for Chevrolet after an argument with Henry Ford I. "Big Bill" had built Chevrolet into a Ford-beater in the Twenties. His son, who had made Pontiac number-three before taking over as Chevrolet general

Where to take the Mustang after 1968 was very much on the minds of Dearborn stylists in July 1966. This styling study is badged Maverick, but the 428 badges clearly indicate this was to be a muscular Mustang. The design was different on either side. It's probably a good thing this car never made it to production!

manager in 1961, now tried to make Ford more competitive with Chevy for the Seventies. Rumors of a drastic shakeup in Ford management began flying almost as soon as Bunkie arrived. Although some staff changes were made, he didn't instigate a wholesale cleanout, and he certainly had Ford looking a lot more competitive.

Knudsen's presidency meant a renaissance for the performance Mustang. He favored lower, sleeker cars, particularly fastbacks. "The long-hood/short-deck concept will continue," Knudsen promised, but "there will be a trend toward designing cars for specific segments of the market." While he denied Ford had any intention of building a sports car, he did hint that a mid-engine experimental was being developed. (This turned out to be the Mach 2, a

one-off exercise begun in 1966 making liberal use of off-the-shelf Mustang components in a curvy two-seat coupe package.) Knudsen also assured the press that Ford's efforts in stock-car racing would continue.

Bunkie was optimistic about the Mustang's market prospects and was not at all bothered by the car's declining sales since 1966. "We are comparing today's Mustang penetration with the penetration of the Mustang when there was no one else in that particular segment of the market. Today [that market is] much more competitive."

One of Knudsen's more productive raids on his former employer resulted in the hiring of Larry Shinoda to head Ford's Special Design Center. Assisting him was

a talented crew that included Harvey Winn, Ken Dowd, Bill Shannon, and Dick Petit. Together with engineers like Chuck Mountain and Ed Hall, Shinoda's department conceived a bevy of eye-opening cars like the King Cobra, a racing Torino fastback.

Shinoda's move to Ford was also good for Mustang. Since the early Sixties, he'd designed wind-cheating shapes such as the original Sting Ray, Corvette Mako Shark, Monza GT, and Corvair Super Spyder for GM's William L. Mitchell. Shinoda was fond of aerodynamic aids—spoilers, low noses, airfoils, front air dams and the like—and some of these would appear on later Mustangs and other Ford models.

Still, Shinoda, like Knudsen, arrived too late to have much impact on the '69 Mustang, whose styling originated in

The Mach 1 show car seen in the previous chapter was restyled, particularly in the front, in time for the 1968 auto show circuit. The major differences are covered headlights and a high-mounted grille more akin to the original 1965-66 Mustang. The quad exhausts have also been split into two groups of three, much like Mustang taillights. Ford used this car to test the waters for the production Mach 1 that was scheduled to bow in 1969.

studies dating as early as October 1965. From the first, Ford designers seemed determined to blow up their ponycar into a mini-Thunderbird, contemplating billowy contours set off by luxury-car touches like knife-edge fenderlines (no doubt inspired by the success of period Lincoln Continentals) and hidden head-lamps. During 1966, in fact, a series of drawings was mandated to get some "Thunderbird influence" into the program. Judging from the factory's photographic records, we can be grateful that effort was abandoned.

But then just as quickly, Ford went the other way, toward an all-out muscle car. This reached fruition in October 1966 with a full-size fastback clay bearing a severely chopped tail, a high-riding rear-fender scoop just aft of each door, and a lengthy hood capped by a huge square grille. As then Mustang design chief Gail Halderman told author Gary Witzenburg: "We went through a period where we were chopping about six inches off the back. But then we went to two inches and finally back to where we started, because we still had to package a spare tire, fuel tank, and some luggage room back there." This mockup quickly led to a less exaggerated exercise that ultimately produced the '69 version of the 2+2, renamed "SportsRoof."

Ford was still toying with additional Mustang body types in this period, full-size tape drawings being made of a fastback wagon and targa-top convertible. The former had a tall "Kamm" tail, like the aforementioned fastback, plus extreme rear-fender "hop-up"; the latter's lower body was more flowing, almost GM-like. Though the targa was abandoned, the wagon went as far as a full-scale fiberglass model showing slightly different treatments on each side. Photographed in the Styling Center auditorium in November 1966, it was a pretty thing, and its front-end profile

In October of 1966 Ford designers were toying with the idea of a Mustang station wagon. It was badged Aspen (*opposite, top*) and was similar in concept to the Volvo sport wagon (and a later Pontiac show car). The 1969 Mustang lineup consisted of six models, among them the fastback coupe (*bottom*) and (*this page*) the luxury-oriented Grandé coupe (*top*), convertible (*center*), and the performance-oriented Mach 1 fastback.

foreshadowed production 1971 styling, but it, too, was doomed. With all that had gone before, a Mustang wagon was a contradiction in terms.

All this effort toward a more impressive ponycar resulted in a '69 Mustang with dimensions that marked a complete departure from the original concept. Overall length went up four inches, most of it in front overhang on the unchanged wheelbase, and the new car was slightly lower and wider. Its face was familiar, but two extra headlights were added outboard of the main grille cavity, a substitute for the mostly ineffective foglights of previous GT models. The old side sculpturing was erased, but rear fenders now bulged noticeably above the wheelarches. Taillights were still vertical clusters but no longer recessed in the tail panel, which was now flat instead of concave, and fastbacks acquired flip-out rear quarter windows. Driving range was increased by enlarging the fuel tank from 17 to 20 gallons.

Dimensional increases were evident inside, too. Thinner doors improved front shoulder room by 2.5 inches and hiproom by 1.5 inches. A modified frame crossmember under the front seat allowed a significant 2.5-inch gain in rear legroom. Cargo capacity was enlarged "13 to 29 percent," according to bubbly Ford press releases, but this really didn't amount to

The Grandé was intended to be as grand as the name implied since it served as the luxury Mustang in 1969. Upmarket touches included a vinyl roof, twin color-keyed exterior mirrors, wire wheel covers, a two-tone paint stripe just below the beltline, and bright wheel well, rocker panel, and rear deck moldings.

much because there'd been so little space before. Even this larger trunk could only manage a two-suiter and not much else.

Mustang's three basic body types continued—hardtop, fastback, and convertible —but there were several new permutations. Two appeared at the beginning of the model year, the third at mid-season.

Taking careful aim at the personal-luxury ponycar represented by Mercury's Cougar and the Pontiac Firebird, Ford released the six- and eight-cylinder Mustang Grandé hardtop. Priced at about $230 over the standard issue, it offered a vinyl-covered roof with identifying script, twin color-keyed door mirrors, wire-wheel covers, a two-tone paint stripe just below the beltline, and bright wheelwell, rocker panel, and rear deck moldings. Dash and door panels were decorated with imitation teakwood trim (a very good copy of the real thing) and its body was hushed by some 55 extra pounds of sound insulation.

Far more exciting was the Mach 1 fastback. A $3139 intruder into Shelby territory, it wore simulated rear-quarter air scoops, decklid spoiler, and a functional hood scoop. The last was nicknamed "The Shaker" by Ford engineers, because it attached to the engine air cleaner and stuck up through a hole in the hood, where it vibrated madly, especially at high revs. Though its dimensional deviations from

other Mustangs were slight, the Mach 1 was definitely the raciest of the new breed. Its broad, flat hood and sweeping "Sports-Roof" combined with NASCAR-style hood tie-downs and that aggressive scoop to create the aura of genuine performance. And with a standard 351-cubic-inch V-8 producing 250 horsepower, it didn't disappoint.

The 351 was developed to fill the rather obvious displacement gap that had existed

in Ford's corporate engine lineup. Descended directly from the original 1962 small-block, it was basically a 302 with the same 4.00-inch bore and a half-inch-longer stroke (3.50 inches). As author Phil Hall observed in *Fearsome Fords*, actual displacement worked out to 351.86 cid, but the company called it "351" to avoid confusion with the 352 Y-block of the late Fifties.

Note that we're talking here about the

Opposite page: The '69 Mustang soft top started at $2849. The GT Equipment Group was still available for $147 with a V-8, which in the case of the 351 added another $189 to the bottom line. *This page*: Probably the most unusual '69 Mustang of all is this pink convertible that has been fitted with a rumble seat. Getting in and out must be a chore, but think of the fun it must be once there!

351 "Windsor" engine, not the more famous "Cleveland" unit. The former got its nickname from the Canadian plant that built it starting in the fall of 1968, a full year before Cleveland production began (in Ohio). While both used the same bore/stroke dimensions, the Windsor featured increased bulkhead strength, a deck height raised 1.27 inches, and a new crankshaft with larger main and crankpin journals. Its intake manifold was of drop-center design, and its valvetrain included "positive-stop" rocker arm studs. Its 4.38-inch bore spacing, as in the original Fairlane 221, was retained for the Cleveland, which became the basis for nearly all of Dearborn's high-performance cars from 1970 through 1974. That relegated the Windsor to a secondary role, used mainly with low compression and two-barrel carburetion.

Ford spent some $100 million in tooling the Cleveland. Its block casting was unique, with an integral timing chain chamber and water crossover passage at the front. Its deck height was exactly one inch higher than the 302's block. Cylinder heads

differed dramatically from the Windsor's, with valves canted 9.5 degrees from the cylinder axis for modified-wedge-type combustion chambers. In addition, the intakes were tilted 4 degrees, 15 minutes forward and the exhaust valves 3 degrees backward for shorter port areas with more

direct gas flow. The widest possible spacing was chosen for maximum valve size. Intakes had a 2.19-inch head diameter, while the forged-steel exhausts were 1.71 inches across their aluminized heads.

Sixes also got their share of attention this year with "center percussion" (forward located) engine mounts that greatly improved operating smoothness. Competition manager Jacque Passino was optimistic about the six-cylinder Mustang: "We've been putting [them out] kind of artificially since '64 to fill up production schedules when we couldn't get V-8s. I think there is a real market for an inexpensive hop-up kit for the 250-cubic-inch engine." But he was whistling in the wind. A kit never materialized, nor did a fuel-injected six he also predicted, though both probably should have.

V-8 offerings for '69 began with the 220-bhp 302 small-block and ran to the top-line 428 Cobra Jet, available with or without ram-air induction and conservatively rated in each case at 335 bhp. Naturally, the Mach 1's 351 was optional

Aside from the Boss 302, the Mach 1 (*right*) was the most expensive model in the '69 line at $3139. It came with the 250-bhp 351 V-8 standard, but it could be optioned with the 335-bhp Cobra Jet 428 (*left*) for $224, or $357 with Ram Air induction. *Car Life* coaxed a 428 Mach 1 from 0-60 mph in 5.5 seconds and covered the quarter-mile in 13.9 seconds at 103.32 mph.

for lesser Mustangs and, indeed, most other Fords except the Falcon and the T-Bird.

For all-out performance, the Cobra Jet was king. Developed by Ford's Light Vehicle Powertrain Department under Tom Feaheny, it made the Mach 1 one of the world's fastest cars. For this application it was thoughtfully combined with a tuned suspension designed by engineer Matt Donner, who used the basic 1967 heavy-

duty setup but mounted one shock ahead of the rear axle line and the other behind it to reduce axle tramp in hard acceleration. Result: a street machine that handled like a Trans-Am racer. The big-engine Mustang still exhibited final oversteer, but the rear end was easily controllable with the accelerator.

"The first Cobra Jets we built were strictly for drag racing," Feaheny said. "The '69s had a type of the competition suspension we offered in '67. Wheel hop was damped out by staggering the rear shocks. It was not a new idea, but it worked. Another thing was the [Goodyear] Polyglas tire. I really can't say enough about this....In '69 every Wide-Oval tire we offered featured Polyglas construction."

All this talk of handling may obscure the matter of straightline performance. The Cobra Jet Mach 1 would run the quarter-

mile in about 13.5 seconds, as quick as the fastest four-seater in production at the time.

With styling help from Shinoda, Ford released an even more exotic Mustang in early 1969, the Boss 302. It was created primarily to compete with the Camaro Z-28 in the Sports Car Club of America's Trans-American Sedan Championship, a road-racing series for production ponycars and compact sedans initiated in 1966. Ford had considered calling it Trans-Am, but Pontiac copped that handle for its hottest '69 Firebird.

Ford had to build 1000 copies to qualify the Boss 302 as production, but ended up turning out 1934 of the '69s. Despite even that limited number, the Boss brought people into Ford showrooms like the original Mustang had back in 1964. Knudsen knew what grabbed the public.

Shinoda's interest in "airflow manage-

A '69 Mach I was available only as a fastback, and it cost almost $300 more than the Mustang ragtop. Enthusiasts liked it because of its racy looks: racing stripes, simulated rear-quarter air scoops, decklid spoiler, functional hood scoop, and NASCAR-style hood tie-downs. They liked it even better, however, for the standard V-8 power and the firmer, tauter suspension. Buyers snapped up 72,458 copies the first year.

ment" was evident in the Boss 302's front and rear spoilers, effective at any speed over 40 mph. The four-inch deep front spoiler was angled forward to direct air around the car. The rear spoiler was an adjustable, inverted airfoil. Matte-black rear window slats *à la* Lamborghini Miura did nothing to enhance airflow but looked terrific. The aerodynamic aids resulted in a gain of perhaps 2.5 seconds per lap at Riverside Raceway in California with no increase in engine power.

Of course, there *was* an increase in power—a big one. The Boss 302's special high-output (H.O.) V-8 was said to produce 290 bhp at 4600 rpm, but estimates of actual output ranged as high as 400 bhp. It employed "Cleveland" heads with oversize 2.33-inch intake valves and 1.71-inch exhaust valves, which were inclined in the big ports to improve fuel flow. Other H.O. tweaks ran to an aluminum high-riser manifold, Holley four-barrel carburetor, dual-point ignition, solid lifters, four-bolt central main bearing caps, forged crankshaft, and special pistons. To help prolong engine life, Ford fitted an ignition cutout that interrupted current flow from the coil to the spark plugs between 5800 and 6000 rpm, thus preventing over-revving.

By 1969, Ford was building the Shelby GT-350 in house. This styling mock-up (*left*) was done in January 1968 in advance of the '69 model year. Mustangs campaigned actively in Trans Am racing (*opposite, bottom*), and this led directly to the limited edition Boss 302 (*this page*). At $3588 it was expensive, but it was the closest thing to a racer one could find in a showroom. Only 1934 '69s were built.

Boss 302 hardware also included ultra-stiff springs, staggered shocks, a four-speed gearbox pulling a shortish 3.50:1 final drive (Detroit "Locker" differentials were available with ratios of 3.50, 3.91 and 4.30:1), power brakes with 11.3-inch-diameter front discs and heavy-duty rear drums, and F60 X 15 Goodyear Polyglas tires. Traction-Lok limited-slip diff was optional, as were Autolite "inline" four-barrel carbs on a special "Cross Boss" manifold. Ford hadn't missed a trick. Even wheel wells were radiused to accept extra-wide racing rubber. On the street, the Boss was unmistakable, with matte-black paint on hood and grille extensions, plus bold bodyside C-stripes with "Boss 302" lettering. It was the ultimate '69 Mustang.

Not counting the Boss 429, that is. This big-block brute was born of Ford's desire to qualify its new semi-hemi 429 V-8 for competition in NASCAR (National Association for Stock Car Automobile Racing). The rules said it had to be installed in 500 production cars, but didn't specify which models. So although the NASCAR racers were Torinos, Ford decided to side-step the rules by putting a street version of the new engine in the smaller Mustang. This *was* Knudsen's doing—Bunkie loved stock-car racing—and quite mad, but glorious.

Besides semi-hemispherical combustion chambers—"crescent-shaped" in Ford

parlance—the Boss 429 engine employed thinwall block construction, aluminum heads, beefed-up main bearings, and a cross-drilled steel-billeted crankshaft. There were actually two versions of this "820" engine: a hydraulic-lifter "S" unit fitted to the first 279 cars, and the later "T" edition, with different rods and pistons and either mechanical or hydraulic lifters. Both were nominally rated at 360 bhp in street form or 375 bhp in race trim. But as with the

H.O. 302, this was just to avoid raising the ire of insurance companies, which were then raising premiums for muscle cars of all kinds.

The semi-hemi was too large for even the '69 Mustang's bigger engine bay, so Ford farmed out Boss 429 assembly to Kar Kraft, a low-volume specialty constructor in Brighton, Michigan. There, a mini-assembly line was set up to shoehorn the engines into selected SportsRoof fastbacks, which required modifying front suspension and inner fender wells, adding diagonal braces twixt wheelhouses and firewall (to resist body twisting in hard acceleration), and moving the battery to the trunk (with the big-block installed, there was no room for it up front). For good measure, track was widened at each end (to 59.5 inches), and wheelarches were flared to accommodate F60 X 15 tires on seven-inch-wide Magnum 500 wheels.

Other features unique to the Boss 429 included a big, functional hood scoop, specific front spoiler, and an engine oil

The mission of the Boss 429 (*both pages*) was quite different from that of the Boss 302, which was developed for Trans Am racing. The Boss 429 was built to homologate Ford's new big-block 429 V-8 for NASCAR tracks, where it would be used in the big Fords. But Mustang needed the publicity and the rules allowed it, so the engine got its workout in the Boss 429.

BOSS 429

KK 429 NASCAR 2465

cooler. Power steering and brakes were standard, as was a Traction-Lok limited-slip differential with 3.91 gearing, to help get all that torque to the pavement. (A Detroit No-Spin axle was optional.) Outside, the Boss 429 was far more subdued than either its small-block brother or the Mach 1: just discreet ID decals and a Boss 302-style rear wing.

For what amounted to a factory drag racer, the Boss 429 was surprisingly lush. Every one left Kar Kraft with the Decor Group that was optional on other Mustangs, along with high-back bucket seats,

deluxe seatbelts, center console and wood-grain dash trim. Ford also threw in the optional Visibility Group, comprising parking brake warning lamp, glovebox lock, and lights for luggage compartment, ashtray, and glovebox. Automatic transmission and air conditioning weren't available even as options.

At $4798, the Boss 429 was the costliest non-Shelby Mustang to date, which may explain why just 852 were called for. Only another 505 would be built to 1970 specs. A tamer 429 then became a regular Mustang option.

The '69 Boss 429 carried its battery in the trunk for better weight distribution (*right*), but that was hardly enough to offset the heft of the big 429 V-8 up front. Since it had to be specially built—by Kar Kraft in Brighton, Michigan—in order to shoehorn the engine in, it cost a whopping $4798. Only 852 were built for 1969, and every one of the remaining examples is a desirable collector's item today.

131

Of course, neither Boss was intended to make money; these were, instead, specialty models that had to be built to appease racing authorities. *Car Life* magazine tested both Bosses and found the little guy quicker to 60 mph—6.9 seconds versus 7.2. But the 302 lost in the quarter-mile at 14.85 seconds and 96.14 mph compared with 14.09 seconds and 102.85 mph for the 429. Top speed for both was shown as 118 mph. Obviously, the 429 was potent, but its chassis was simply overwhelmed in standing-start acceleration. As a starting point for those who wished to modify for the strip, it was fearsome, but on the street it was something of a disappointment.

Not so the Boss 302, and it's interesting to note that the example tested by *Car Life* turned in the same quarter-mile time as the magazine's Camaro Z-28. *Car and Driver* pronounced the Boss 302 "the best handling Ford ever....[It] may just be the new standard by which everything from Detroit must be judged....It's what the Shelby GT-350s and 500s should have been but weren't." All of which made for something of a bargain, even at a not-inexpensive $3588.

Mustang's expansion into the luxury and performance ends of the ponycar field showed interesting results. Out of 184,000

cars delivered in the first half of 1969, only about 15,000 were Grandés but close to 46,000 were Mach 1s. On cue, division general manager John Naughton predicted "heavy emphasis on performance" for what he (or his press writers) termed the "Sizzlin' '70s."

The Boss 302 reappeared for 1970, now priced at $3720. It received the new front end of the regular Mustangs, which reverted to single headlights. The 302 was rated at 290 bhp, but some observers estimated that the truth was closer to 400. Boss 302 output increased to 6319 units in 1970.

The 1970 Mach 1 featured ribbed lower body trim that included a Mach 1 logo. Engine choices remained basically the same, except that the 428 option was replaced by a 429 during the model run. Output fell to 40,970 units.

"We're going to be where the action is," Naughton declared, "and we're going to have the hardware to meet the action requirements of buyers everywhere." The Mach 1, he said, would remain Ford's big gun in the performance race. The Bosses 302 and 429 were for the outer fringes of the market—and the Trans-Am. Two Boss styling features, backlight louvers and adjustable rear spoiler, proved so popular that they became options for any 1970 SportsRoof. Ford, said Naughton, was going to "make it happen in 1970."

And in a way, Ford did. That year's Boss 302, as *Motor Trend* put it, was "even Bossier." Unique side striping identified it; a well-engineered suspension cornered it; and hotter than ever engines powered it. A new item was a Hurst competition shifter with T-handle, the first Hurst linkage in a production Mustang. Further up the price scale, at around $5000, was the Boss 429 with the Cobra Jet NASCAR engine. Again there were two versions: the 820T, essentially unchanged from late '69, and a new 820A with minor adjustments to its

Thermactor emissions-control system, a sign of the times.

Mach 1 powerplants ranged from the standard two-barrel 351 with 250 bhp to the four-barrel 428 with ram air, still at its token 335-bhp rating. The Cleveland engine was further improved by larger intake and exhaust ports. Mach 1 handling was helped by addition of a rear stabilizer bar that allowed the use of more moderate spring rates for a better ride.

This year's Mach 1 got its own special grille with driving lamps. The GT Equip-

The 1970 fastback (*both pages*) was referred to as the "SportsRoof." It wasn't as popular as the notchback coupe body style, but it was popular with those who didn't have the extra $500 it took to buy a Mach 1. Of course, options like the four-barrel 351 V-8 (*right*) at $93 ate into the price differential. The "C" side stripes were popular, giving the car a bit of a "Boss" look. SportsRoof production came to 39,316 units for the 1970 model year.

ment Group was still included, but the package itself was eliminated as a separate option for other Mustangs, leaving enthusiastic drivers to be content with the Competition Suspension Package. The latter was now offered in two forms. One was for four-barrel 351 and 428 V-8s with automatic. The other, for manual-shift 428 cars, had staggered shocks. New among 1970 option groups was the Drag Pack, available only with the 428 engine and comprising stronger con rods, heavy-duty oil cooler, and a modified rotating assembly. Detroit No-Spin differential was still on the order form with gearing as short as 4.30:1, so buyers who wanted to go like blazes could still do so in a suitably optioned 1970 Mustang.

The luxury Grandé returned with either six or V-8 power. Like other Mustangs this year, it inherited the Mach 1's high-back front bucket seats, which added greatly to interior comfort. A landau-style black or white vinyl roof, twin racing-type door mirrors, special identification, and bright wheel lip moldings completed the package as before.

The Mustang had "matured" by 1970. It still rode a 108-inch wheelbase, but it was bigger all the way around and weighed about 300 pounds more than the original. A 220-bhp 302 V-8 was the most popular engine choice, as on the car above. A half-vinyl roof (*left*) was a popular option at $84. Mustang persisted with its triple-taillight theme (*right*).

There were still "basic" Mustangs in 1970, available with standard six or 302 V-8 in hardtop, convertible, and Sports-Roof fastback body styles. Like other models, they boasted new front-end styling marked by the return of single headlights. Rear appearance was revised with recessed taillamps, and minor ornamentation was shuffled across the line. Prices hadn't climbed much since the Mustang's early days. The six-cylinder hardtop still listed at only a bit more than $2700, the V-8 convertible for as little as $3126.

Convertibles, though, were on the wane throughout Detroit, and the number of open Mustangs built was only about 7700 this year. Continued buyer preference for air conditioning and closed bodies had conspired to reduce the popularity of convertibles, including Mustang's.

Though touted as the number-one ponycar, Mustang faced more competition than ever for 1970. The beefy new Dodge Challenger and a completely redone Plymouth Barracuda companion appeared to do battle, followed at mid-season by the handsome second-generation Chevrolet Camaro/Pontiac Firebird. So despite the same diverse and exciting model group as in '69, Mustang model year volume fell alarmingly to 190,727 units, down from nearly 300,000. Though this partly reflected the shrinking demand for pony-cars in general, Mustang's design familiarity was also to blame. Fastbacks slipped 40 percent, hardtops declined 35 percent. While the Mach 1 accounted for a solid proportion of fastback sales, it was not a high-volume item by mid-Sixties standards and couldn't make up for continuing strong competition from other performance models from Ford and rival manufacturers. The Boss 302 remained strictly a limited-production Trans-Am special with low sales potential: output was just 6319 units.

But bigger things were coming—literally. Bunkie was about to have his day with a new-generation Ford ponycar that would be like no Mustang before—or, thankfully, since.

The 1970 Mustang convertible retailed for $3025, about $500 more than the '65. But whereas the '65 ragtop accounted for over 100,000 sales in that long model year, only 7673 were built for 1970. That, of course, makes them all the more desirable now.

1969-70 MUSTANG AT A GLANCE

Model Year Production

No.	Model	1969	1970
63A	Fastback, standard	56,022	39,470
63B	Fastback, deluxe	5,958	6,464
63C	Fastback, Mach 1	72,458	40,970
65A	Hardtop, standard	118,613	77,161
65B	Hardtop, deluxe	5,210	5,408
65C	Hardtop, bench seats	4,131	—
65D	Hardtop, deluxe bench seat	504	—
65E	Hardtop, Grandé	22,182	13,581
76A	Convertible, standard	11,307	6,199
76B	Convertible, deluxe	3,439	1,474
	TOTAL	299,824	190,727

Prices/Weights
($/lbs)

		1969	1970
01	Hardtop, I-6	$2635/2690	$2721/2721
02	Fastback, I-6	$2635/2713	$2771/2745
03	Convertible, I-6	$2849/2800	$3025/2831
04	Grandé hardtop, I-6	$2866/2765	$2926/2806
01	Hardtop, V-8	$2740/2906	$2822/2923
02	Fastback, V-8	$2740/2930	$2872/2947
02	Boss 302 fastback, V-8	$3588/3210	$3720/3227
03	Convertible, V-8	$2954/3016	$3126/3033
04	Grandé, V-8	$2971/2981	$3028/3008
05	Mach 1 fastback, V-8	$3139/3175	$3271/3240

General Specifications

	1969	1970
Wheelbase (in.)	108.0	108.0
Overall length (in.)	187.4	187.4
Overall width (in.)	71.3	71.7
Std. Trans.	3-sp. man.	3-sp. man.
Optional Trans.	4-sp. man. 3-sp. auto.	4-sp. man. 3-sp. auto.

Engine Availability

Type	cid	bhp	1969	1970
I-6	200	115/120	Std.	Std.
I-6	250	155	Opt.	Opt.
V-8	302	220	Std.[1]	Std.[1]
V-8	351	250	Opt.[2]	Opt.[2]
V-8	351	290/300	Opt.	Opt.
V-8	390	320	Opt.	—
V-8	428	335	Opt.	Opt.
V-8	428	335[3]	Opt.	Opt.
V-8	429	375[4]	Opt.	Opt.

1 290 bhp std. Boss 302
2 std. Mach 1
3 with Ram Air
4 Boss 429 only

141

CHAPTER SIX

1971-73:
From
Quarter Horse
to
Clydesdale

A fter less than two years as Ford Motor Company president, Bunkie Knudsen was summarily dismissed in late 1969. Chairman Henry Ford II simply said that "things just didn't work out," though he never elaborated on that in line with his longtime motto, "never complain, never explain."

Insiders, however, suggested that, like his father before him, Knudsen had accumulated, and was wielding, too much power. "Knudsen moved in and started doing things his way," wrote prominent Detroit analyst Robert W. Irvin. "Knudsen was almost running the company and [some said] he had alienated many other top executives. Others said Knudsen's departure was an indication of how the Fords don't like to share power." Irvin wrote

those words in July 1978 as a comment on the firing of Lee A. Iacocca.

To soften the impact of Knudsen's dismissal, HF II announced a presidential troika comprising R.L. Stevenson for International Operations, R.J. Hampson for Non-Automotive Operations, and Iacocca for North American Operations.

But that lasted only a year: Iacocca became overall president in 1970.

By late 1969, it had become clear the ponycar was losing its appeal. Mustang sales had been sliding since '67. Camaro and Firebird were holding up but not gaining. The AMC Javelin was a mild success but no blockbuster. Neither were

the rebodied 1970 Plymouth Barracuda and its new Dodge stablemate, the aptly named Challenger, which did not bring in the pile of orders Chrysler had expected. By 1971, compacts like the Ford Pinto and Maverick, Chevrolet Vega and AMC Gremlin were cutting into ponycar sales, which were down to almost half of what

they'd been in their best-ever year, 1967.

Given the auto industry's normal lead time, the '71 Mustang was really shaped by the events of 1968-69 — and by Bunkie Knudsen. Iacocca didn't have nearly as much to do with it. Foremost among the influences was a cold, hard fact that Ford found hard to ignore: "Total Performance"

Opposite page: Styling studies in 1968 and '69 went off in different directions. The Cobra (*top*) predicted early '70s styling; the Apex (*center row*) tried a two-seater format. The Maverick (*bottom*) looked a lot like the real thing. The 302 Mustang (*this page*) was an early study in the 1974 Mustang II program.

was no longer the sales-booster it once was. The effect of impending new government regulations was a hotly debated unknown, and the idea that the world might soon be short of oil was not yet taken seriously in many quarters. With all this, product planners concluded that lack of sufficient interior space was the reason ponycars started trailing compacts in sales, so the decision to make the next-generation Mustang larger, roomier and heavier was perfectly logical in the context of the late Sixties.

Bigger the '71 definitely was: as big as a Mustang would ever get, in fact. An agile quarter horse had become a lumbering Clydesdale. Styling work began as early as May 1967, about nine months before Knudsen arrived in Dearborn. Most clay models produced through early '68 were heavy-looking to the point of ungainliness —typically rounded and Thunderbird-ish, often clumsy. Designers eventually stripped away the flab, opting for crisp, almost severely creased lines married to swoopy fender shapes and kicked-up "ducktails." By mid-June of '68, the basic elements of the final production design were more or less in place—with Knudsen's blessing, of course.

The result was a Mustang ballooned eight inches in overall length, six inches in width, and some 600 pounds in curb weight, though wheelbase was upped only an inch. The familiar long-hood/short-deck proportions were retained, but the car was more "styled" than ever, aping Ford's GT Le Mans racers—and the tastes of Knudsen and Larry Shinoda (who'd depart Dearborn when Bunkie did).

Most noticeable were a sweeping, almost horizontal fastback roofline, a full-width grille and Kamm-style back panel inspired by the Shelby-Mustangs (abandoned after 1970), and a more acute windshield angle and hidden wipers (reflecting Shinoda's GM background). The advent of color-

This page: The Mach 1 (*top and second from top*) was also part of the 1974 Mustang II program. The Milano (*third from top*) was displayed in 1970; it previewed the 1971 fastback theme. *Opposite page*: The '71 Mustang Mach 1 received new styling on a 109-inch wheelbase. The top 351 V-8 option was good for 330 bhp. Other 351s yielded 240 and 285 bhp.

keyed, polyurethane-covered bumpers made the front end even more interesting and better integrated. This was standard on Mach 1, along with a special twin-scoop hood (optional on other models) and a unique grille with a small running-horse emblem on honeycomb mesh, flanked by horizontal parking lamps styled to look like driving lights. On other Mustangs, the rectangular opening was graced by the return of the chrome-framed horse and horizontal divider bar. Ironically, and though nobody could have predicted it in 1968, Ford would be out of racing only a few months after this racy new styling appeared, abandoning most of its efforts in Trans-Am, USAC, NASCAR, and international competition in late 1970.

More stringent emissions standards took a toll on Mustang's 1971 engine lineup. The Boss 302's H.O. V-8 was replaced by a Boss 351 Cleveland with four-barrel carburetor, 11.0:1 compression ratio, and 330 horsepower (gross) at 5400 rpm. It was more tractable than the H.O. and, since it wasn't as high-revving, more durable. On other Mustangs, the standard V-8 was a 302, with two-barrel carb and 9.0:1 compression yielding 210 bhp at 4600 rpm. The base six was now the 250

The '71 Boss 351 featured Ram Air induction and 330 horsepower. It sold for $4124 and weighed 3227 pounds. Like the earlier Boss Mustangs, it came as a complete package with few options; 1971 would be the last year for the Boss.

truck mill with 9.0:1 compression and 145 bhp at 4000 rpm. There were three other optional V-8s: a two-barrel 351 with 240 gross horses, a four-barrel version with 285, and the new four-barrel 429 Cobra Jet, replacing the previous 428 big-blocks and rated at 370 bhp with or without Ram Air induction. There was also a Super Cobra Jet boasting 375 bhp, which made even the weightier '71 a real screamer, though it garnered few orders.

Though ostensibly a performance machine as before, the Mach 1 could still be ordered with air conditioning ($407) and automatic transmission ($238), as well as a slew of convenience features more appropriate to a luxury car: power steering, tilt steering wheel, "sport deck" rear seat, AM/FM stereo, and intermittent wipers. Other extra-cost items included sports interior ($130), power front disc brakes ($70), center console ($60), and instrument group ($54).

In fact, liberal use of the option book could raise the Mach 1's $3268 base price to well over $5500. Standard equipment this year included high-back bucket seats,

Opposite page: The base six-cylinder Mustang coupe sold for $2911 in 1971, but goodies like the big V-8 with Ram Air induction and sporty wheels added $500 to the sticker. The hardtop coupe was the most popular model with 65,696 built. *This page*: The convertible continued to lose favor with buyers as production dipped to only 6121 units. It was priced at $3227; the 302 V-8 developed 210 horsepower at 4600 rpm.

integrated front spoiler, honeycomb grille, dual exhausts, auxiliary lamps, and racing-style door mirrors. The 429CJ engine cost $436 extra and made the Mach 1 undeniably quick. So equipped, the car would do 0-60 mph in 6.5 seconds, 0-75 in about 9.0 seconds, and the quarter-mile in 14.5 seconds. With automatic transmission and 3.25:1 final drive ratio, top speed was

about 115 mph, fuel "economy" 10-11 mpg. "It is a decent mixture for those who want good performance and some comfort," wrote Chuck Koch in *Motor Trend* magazine, "but it still remains a little unwieldy for city traffic."

That larger, high-output small-block we mentioned was the heart of this year's new Boss 351 fastback, which replaced the Bosses 302 and 429 as the racer's Mustang. Aside from name decals, special mid-flank striping, and Boss-style front spoiler, it looked much like the Mach 1. Koch tested this one too and found it handled better than the Mach 1, thanks to a standard "competition" suspension with uprated coil springs and hydraulic shocks up front, staggered rear shocks, and front and rear stabilizer bars. The Boss 351 also proved quicker than Koch's Mach 1 429, capable of 0-60 mph in 5.8 seconds and the quarter-mile in 13.8 seconds. However, a short 3.91:1 rear axle limited top speed to only about 100 mph.

The 210-bhp 302 was naturally no match for these very powerful V-8s. Its typical figures were 0-60 mph in 10 seconds, the quarter-mile in 17.5 seconds, and a top speed of only 86 mph (with 2.79:1 axle ratio and automatic). Yet this was hardly sluggish, and the 302 delivered

The 1971 and '72 Mustang Mach 1s were almost identical, although the 429 V-8 was dropped for '72. The standard engine was the 302 V-8, rated at 210 horsepower in 1971, and 141 *net* bhp in 1972. Competition suspension, NASA hood scoops, variable-ratio power steering, and three-speed manual transmission came standard.

decent mileage (up to 17 mpg). All things considered, it was probably this year's best all-around Mustang power choice.

In retrospect, the '71 Mustang doesn't seem like a bad car, though it got a lot of bad press at the time. It was larger because buyers didn't like cars with cramped interiors. It was the thirstiest Mustang yet because, with gas still selling for only 30 cents a gallon, most buyers weren't too concerned about fuel economy. Yet the '71, especially with the competition suspension, rode and handled better than previous Mustangs. Understeer was greatly reduced, and roadholding was improved. New variable-ratio power steering provided better road feel than previous fixed-ratio Mustang systems despite the gains in weight and size. The low, flat-roof fastback was racy-looking and attractive in an era of uninspired styling.

The Grandé (*above*) continued its role as the luxury Mustang for '72. It listed at $2915, almost $200 more than the regular coupe, and came with a standard vinyl roof and unique body stripes. In an effort to hype sales, Ford trotted out springtime Sprint Decor Option specials for the 1972 Pinto, Maverick, and Mustang (*right and opposite*). All were white, with red and blue highlights and prominent U.S.A. decals.

The '72 Mustang convertible could also be ordered with the Sprint Decor Option. Since only 6401 convertibles were built that year, production of the Sprint models had to be low. Base price of the ragtop came in at $3015 and, at 3099 pounds, it was the heaviest model in the lineup.

159

But a good car doesn't necessarily mean good sales, as Ford Motor Company knew all too well. If Mustang wasn't losing customers to Camaro, Firebird, and Barracuda, it was definitely being outsold by the Maverick, Plymouth Valiant, Dodge Dart, and Chevrolet Nova. So even though it was all-new, Mustang once again sagged in sales. Model year '71 production totaled less than 150,000, hardtops dropping to 83,000, the convertible capturing a bit more than 6000 and the fastback holding at about 60,000. Included in the last are an estimated 1800 copies of the Boss 351, which was dropped at mid-season (there was little need for it once Ford gave up racing). As you might guess, it's the most collectible '71 Mustang today.

There's little to do with a one-year-old design in Detroit but live with it, and that's precisely what Ford did with Mustang for 1972. Even stricter emission standards dictated detuning the standard six and eight as well as the three optional 351 V-8s.

Ironically enough, the big-block 429, a major reason for the 1971's size increase, was eliminated.

Like other Detroit automakers, Ford switched to quoting horsepower in SAE net, rather than gross, measure for 1972. The six was thus more accurately rated at 95 bhp, the 302 V-8 at 136 bhp, and the 351s from 168 to 275 bhp. The last applied to a detuned Boss 351 unit called 351 H.O., a late addition to the option chart.

With so little new or really exciting in the '72 Mustang, Ford resorted to promoting new colors and fabrics. Among the prettiest was the Sprint Decor Option, available for hardtop and SportsRoof

Opposite page: Although the early Mustangs came with full-disc hubcaps as standard equipment, this was not the case in 1972. The coupe retailed for $2729 and, with a production run of 57,350 units, was the most popular model in 1972. *This page*: Although optional, most '72 Mustangs wore full-wheel discs and had a 302 V-8, like the convertible seen here.

models. It could be combined with mag wheels, raised-white-letter tires, and competition suspension. Sprints were usually painted white and had broad, blue Shelby-style facing stripes edged in red. Complementary colors were used inside. "Control and balance make it a beautiful experience," the ads read. Nevertheless, Mustang sales as a whole dipped again, this time by about 20 percent. Only the convertible, which by now didn't account for much of the yearly total, maintained its previous level.

By this time, Ford was well along with development of a totally new Mustang, a car more faithful to the spirit of the original. Typically, the real push for a total redesign

came from Lee Iacocca. "I've said it a hundred times and I'll say it again: the Mustang market never left us, we left it," he would remark later. "We kept the 460 out of it, but we had all the other engines in it." Echoed design vice-president Eugene Bordinat: "We started out with a secretary car and all of a sudden we had a behemoth."

Mustang thus remained its hefty self for one more year, 1973, but sold a bit better. The convertible scored the largest percentage increase—up a resounding 100 percent, to nearly 12,000 units—but only because Ford had announced the body style would be discontinued the next year. The 1973 Mustang convertible was thus the last

ragtop Ford would offer for the next decade.

This year brought the federal government's new impact standards for bumpers, which had to sustain low-speed shunts without damage in the front (and, from '74, the rear too). Many automakers, including Ford, designed some pretty awful-looking cow-catchers to meet this requirement (perhaps out of spite), but Mustang fared better than most '73s, its front bumper sticking out only a little more than in '72 and not looking too bad for it. An I-beam mounting bar inside a box-section bracket attached to two longitudinal rubber blocks that gave way on

The 1973 Mustang sported an altered grille and a trim shuffle. It would be the last year for the "big" Mustangs. The Grandé (*opposite*) listed at $2946 and saw a production run of 25,674 units. The fastback Mach 1 (*this page*) sported new side trim. It was priced at $3088 and output improved by about 25 percent to 35,440 units. Its standard 302 V-8 put out 136 bhp, although a 154/156-bhp 351 was still listed.

contact, then bounced back to their original position. As before, an optional color-keyed rubber cover was available to clean up appearance even more.

The influence of federal requirements was evident elsewhere, too. Mustang's 1973 dash was bereft of sharp knobs and other projections that might cause unnecessary injury in a crash, and got extra padding. Bigger brakes were fitted, as were larger calipers for cars with non-power discs. Flame retardant interior materials were adopted to meet the government's "burn rate" standard of four inches per minute. Emission control was handled by crankcase ventilation and exhaust gas recirculation. The latter routed gases from the exhaust manifold through a vacuum valve into the carburetor, where they were diluted by the incoming fuel/air mixture.

This permitted leaner carburetor settings for lower emissions.

Front bumper aside, the '73 Mustang saw little visual change from 1971-72. As before, Mach 1 nose styling was optionally available on convertibles and hardtops in an exterior Decor Group, where the "sport" parking lamps were turned vertically, a small spotter's point. Mustang was the only '73 Ford offering the division's High-Output 351 V-8. Prices, which had been cut the year before to spark sales, remained fairly stable. The base six-cylinder hardtop listed at $2760, while the V-8 convertible was the most expensive at $3189. The Mach 1 still with the base 351 as standard, sold for $3088.

Nine years after the Mustang's debut, the old marketing technique of offering a wide range of options was still important.

The '73, Ford said, was "designed to be designed by you." And so it was. The optional vinyl top now came in six colors. It covered the whole roof on hardtops and the front three-quarters on fastbacks. A Mach 1-type hood with lock pins and matte silver or black center section was available. Also on the list were forged aluminum wheels, "metallic glow" paint, and decorative side striping. An electric rear window defroster was available for hardtops and SportsRoofs.

And with that came the end of the third-generation Mustang. Though its basic shape, sporty styling, and long option list had endured, Ford's ponycar had grown into something completely different from the 1965 original. Everybody knew that, and by 1973 most agreed that it wasn't the way to go. But Ford was readying an

entirely new product, a concept that would
begin a second revolution: a sporty compact for the brave, if battered, new world
of the Seventies.

Many people knew that 1973 would be the
last year for a Mustang ragtop, so it's not
surprising that sales almost doubled to
11,853 units. It sold for $3102, although a
well-equipped example, like the one seen
here, could nudge $5000. This would also
be the last year, temporarily as it turned
out, that Mustang would offer V-8 engines.

1971-73 MUSTANG AT A GLANCE

Model Year Production

No.	Model	1971	1972	1973
63D	Fastback, standard	23,956	15,622	10,820
63R	Fastback, Mach 1	36,499	27,675	35,440
65D	Hardtop, standard	65,696	57,350	51,480
65F	Hardtop, Grandé	17,406	18,045	25,674
76D	Convertible, standard	6,121	6,401	11,853
	TOTAL	149,678	125,093	134,267

Prices/Weights
($/lbs)

	Models	1971	1972	1973
01	Hardtop, I-6	$2911/2937	$2729/2941	$2760/2995
02	Fastback, I-6	$2973/2907	$2786/2908	$2820/3008
03	Convertible, I-6	$3227/3059	$3015/3051	$3102/3126
04	Grandé hardtop, I-6	$3117/2963	$2915/2965	$2946/3003
01	Hardtop, V-8	$3006/3026	$2816/3025	$2897/3085
02	Fastback, V-8	$3068/2993	$2873/2995	$2907/3098
02	Boss 351 fastback, V-8	$4124/3281	—	—
03	Convertible, V-8	$3320/3145	$3101/3147	$3189/3216
04	Grandé hardtop, V-8	$3212/3049	$3002/3051	$3088/3115
05	Mach 1 fastback, V-8	$3268/3220	$3053/3046	$3088/3115

General Specifications

	1971	1972	1973
Wheelbase (in.)	109.0	109.0	109.0
Overall length (in.)	187.5 (6) 189.5 (8)	190.0	194.0
Overall width (in.)	75.0	75.0	75.0
Std. Trans.	3-sp. man.	3-sp. man.	3-sp. man.
Optional Trans.	4-sp. man. 3-sp. auto.	4-sp. man. 3-sp. auto.	4-sp. man. 3-sp. auto.

Engine Availability

Type	cid	bhp	1971	1972	1973
I-6	250	145 (gross)[1]	Std.	Std.	Std.
V-8	302	210 (gross)[2]	Std.	Std.	Std.
V-8	351	240 (gross)	Opt.	—	—
V-8	351	285 (gross)	Opt.	—	—
V-8	351	280 (gross)	Opt.	—	—
V-8	351	330 (gross)	Std.[3]	—	—
V-8	429	370 (gross)	Opt.	—	—
V-8	351	168 (net)	—	Opt.	Opt.
V-8	351	200 (net)	—	Opt.	Opt.
V-8	351	275 (net)	—	Opt.	Opt.

1 rated 95 hp (net) 1972-73
2 rated 136 hp (net) 1972-73
3 std. Boss 351 only

Although the big Mustangs of 1971-73 were at first shunned by collectors, the more desirable models, like this '73 convertible, are being snapped up quickly these days in spite of rapidly escalating prices. As the biggest Mustangs ever, they ended an era.

CHAPTER SEVEN

1974-78:
Back
to the
Future

In looking to the future by going back to first principles, the smaller and lighter Mustang II began an important new chapter in the Mustang saga. It couldn't have been better timed, arriving in Ford showrooms almost simultaneously with the 1973-74 Energy Crisis, and people came in droves to see it. With 385,993 units in its first year, Mustang II came within 10 percent of the original Mustang's 12-month production record of 418,812 cars.

Lee Iacocca was behind it—again—and those first-year sales made him look pretty good—again. Of course, Mustang II was in the works some time before the Organization of Petroleum Exporting Countries (OPEC) decided to put the squeeze on world oil supplies. That this happened so soon after the car appeared was mere coincidence.

The market changes that had occurred since the days of the original Mustang were already being reflected in more recent Dearborn products. Maverick, introduced in 1970, was dimensionally close to the first Mustang, and topped its debut-year sales record at over 450,000 (again, an extra-long selling season helped). But this was an economy compact, not a sporty car. Mustang II would fill that role.

Though Iacocca had only guessed that a market existed for the original Mustang, he knew *in advance* that demand for Mustang II would be strong. Sporty 2+2

The 1974 Mustang II was a shock to those used to the larger 1971-73 models, although the late-1973 Arab oil embargo probably cushioned the blow. The Mustang II borrowed parts from the subcompact Pinto, but the latter benefited because some of them were upgraded for use on both cars.

import coupes with luxury trim, bucket seats, and four-on-the-floor were increasingly popular in the early Seventies. Ford's own British/German Capri and GM's German-built Opel Manta, both "captive imports," and cars like the Toyota Celica from Japan were all selling well. In 1965 such "mini-ponycars" accounted for less than 100,000 sales but were up to 300,000 by 1972—and projected to go beyond 400,000 for '74. Mustang II's mission was to capture a big slice of this sizeable new pie.

Eugene Bordinat, then vice-president for Ford design, gave the father of the original ponycar full credit for the Mustang II: "Iacocca was the first guy to come along who had the feeling for cars that had existed in General Motors for some time." For his part, Iacocca observed: "When I look at the foreign-car market and see that one in five is a sporty car, I know something's

happening. Look at what the Celica started to do before the two devaluations [of the dollar] nailed it! Anyone who decides to sit this out just ain't gonna dance!"

Nevertheless, Mustang II, like its 1965 forebear, did not spring into being overnight. Because design studies were initiated amidst the muscle-car mania of mid-1969, first thoughts involved mere evolutions of the "fat" 1971-73 generation. If anything, these early proposals were even bigger and

heavier-looking, reflecting Ford's belief that buyers would still want roomy, "impressive" ponycars in the mid-Seventies. But by the time Iacocca became Ford Motor Company president in 1970, the bottom had dropped out of the ponycar market, and the imported Capri, which Iacocca said was more like the original "than any Mustang we have today," was doing land-office business at Lincoln-Mercury dealers.

These events prompted a series of consumer clinics to gauge prospects for a smaller domestically produced sporty car (market research still reigned supreme in Dearborn planning). Favorable reaction there led to two new-model development programs: "Ohio," a Mustang-like car based on the hot-selling Maverick, and "Arizona," an even smaller sportster derived from the new four-cylinder Pinto subcompact set to bow for 1971. But neither effort produced anything that satisfied Iacocca,

Both pages: This series of styling studies from 1970 indicates that the initial thinking for the Mustang II program was simply an extension of 1971-73 concepts, reflecting the influence of the Knudsen regime. In fact, all of the studies seen here were mounted on the 1971-73 109-inch wheelbase. The greenhouse of these studies varied from standard Mustang fare, but the Mustang-style grille and triple-taillight theme were carried over in modified form.

Designing Mustang II
by Dick Nesbitt

After being hired in 1971 by Ford Motor Company as an automotive designer, I relocated from Los Angeles to Dearborn, Michigan, where I went to work at Ford's design center. I thought that Ford's product lines for 1971 and '72 were among their best ever—with strong, well-developed visual images for Ford, Mercury, and the Continental. The 1971 and '72 Mustang convertibles struck me as being appealing and underrated. Still, Mustang seemed to have lost its focus—its image had become blurred. Lee Iacocca, the driving force behind the Mustang's creation, felt that the

car's expansion to intermediate size and weight was one of the worst marketing blunders ever made by the American auto industry. Added to this was the visual horror of government-mandated bumpers, which dominated already-approved designs for Ford's 1973 model year. Mustang needed a new direction, and for inspiration Ford was looking keenly at a number of competing cars, including the Toyota Celica, which—irony of ironies—had itself been inspired by the original Mustang concept.

Designing Mustang II continued:
Genesis

My first assignment as a new designer was to Lincoln-Mercury's production exterior-

design studio, where I worked on proposals for Cougar, Montego, and Comet. Shortly afterward, our studio—as well as others—was asked to present a proposal for an all-new and considerably downsized Mustang II project. Mustang sales had been falling steadily for several years, and Iacocca had decided that the ponycar should return to its original character by model year 1974. To this end, several design studies had been attempted before I joined the company, but Iacocca felt they were all far off the mark. He wanted a concerted effort; I even heard that he had prohibited designers over the age of 30 from working on the project, apparently believing that the older guys didn't have the right "feel" for the

171

Bordinat, or Advanced Design chief Don DeLaRossa.

Then, in November 1970, Ford acquired a controlling interest in Ghia of Italy, and Iacocca wasted no time in asking the famed coachbuilder to submit concepts for the new small sporty car. With typical dispatch, Ghia supplied a running prototype in just 53 days, a slope-nose fastback that greatly accelerated the drive toward the eventual Mustang II. "Aside from the new slant on styling that it gave us," Iacocca said later, "the quick delivery of that real, live, driveable sample...coalesced our thinking and gave us something tangible to look at and argue about early in the game, an experience that I had never had before in my career in the company....It was a great early boost for the whole program."

By mid-1971, management had decided to abandon the Ohio, along with the idea of using the bulky old straight six from the existing Mustang. Bordinat recalled that DeLaRossa "put his studio to work on a clay model showing how big the Mustang would have to be to accommodate that big I-6 engine. He got me to call Lee over for a look at it. Don became, shall we say, very forthright and told Lee that if we really wanted to make a smaller car, we had better start with a smaller engine because this one with this engine in it was getting bigger even before it was designed. Lee agreed with us and that was the end of the I-6. The next thing we heard was that the choice of engines would be a new small 2.3-liter four-cylinder and a larger-displacement version of the German Capri V-6, so we were able to get down to making the rest of the car smaller too."

With that decided, and taking the Arizona project as a starting point, Iacocca staged another friendly intramural design competition of the sort he'd used to stimulate creation of the original Mustang.

"Lee thinks that pitting our guys against each other breeds our best stuff," Bordinat later joked. "I've tried to disagree with him, but every time we do it, we get an exceptionally good car." This contest, begun in August 1971 and ultimately running three months, involved the Ford and L-M production studios, DeLaRossa's Advanced Design group, and the Interior Studio.

Once again, competing teams worked from an idea Iacocca had clearly defined: "The new Mustang must be small, with a wheelbase between 96 and 100 inches. It must be a sporty notchback and/or fastback coupe; the convertible is dead and can be forgotten. [He'd later think otherwise at Chrysler Corporation.] It must come as standard with a four-speed manual gearbox and a four-cylinder or small six-cylinder engine. Most important, it must be luxurious—upholstered in quality materials and carefully built."

Ben Bidwell, who handled Mustang II product planning (and later joined Iacocca at Chrysler, where he's president at this writing), said Iacocca took a personal interest in the quality control aspect: "He will be out there in the showroom and he'll run his finger around the molding, and if it so much as scrapes him, some poor son of a gun will get it."

Of course, Iacocca also took a keen interest in Mustang II styling. As planning chief Hal Sperlich recalled: "He was planning an entirely new kind of domestic car for a different kind of customer, so naturally he wanted it to look different from other cars on the market; different from the Mustangs of 1971, 1972 and 1973; different from the Pinto and different from the Capri, too."

All this ultimately came down to a late-November management review of five full-scale clay models: one notchback and four fastbacks. The hands-down winner was a

fastback from the Lincoln-Mercury group under Al Mueller. Like Joe Oros before him, he painted his proposal—persimmon, no less—to increase his team's chances.

But though surprisingly little altered for production, this design met with mixed reviews, and some felt that the notchback derived from it was a hodge-podge. The

Opposite page: The "Anaheim" proposal by Don DeLaRossa convinced management to include a notchback in the Mustang II program. *This page:* It inspired a Ghia two-seat proposal (*top left*). Closer to what ultimately emerged was another study dated September 23, 1971 (*top right*). A Capri based on the Mustang II was even considered (*above*).

---

image that said performance. He actively encouraged the development of my concept, which the studio staff came to call the "Boss 302" theme.

**Designing Mustang II continued:
A Coupe, Quickly**

The final design proposal to be submitted by our Lincoln-Mercury studio was a three-door fastback-only created by staff designer Howard "Buck" Mook. It was this proposal that was selected by Lee Iacocca over all those from the other studios. Unfortunately, the proposal turned out to be a disappointment to the designers involved in its genesis. The proposed car's exaggeratedly curvaceous lines and heavily dipped beltline

combined with massive non-integrated bumpers and small, 13-inch wheels to create a stubby, overworked appearance. All told, it was a far cry from the sophisticated "domestic Capri" that had been envisioned.

The design received encouraging responses in most markets where it was "clinic'-surveyed, but the lack of a traditional coupe body style was soon perceived as a serious omission. Our Lincoln-Mercury design studio eventually received instructions to create a coupe alternative in the fastest time possible.

**Designing Mustang II continued:
Creation in Clay and Fiberglass**

A few days were spent developing coupe

fastback was considered more handsome, though it wasn't a "classic" shape like the '65' Mustang. It was, however, more practical by dint of its European-style lift-up rear "door," a first for Mustang and another boost to the popularity of hatch-back body styles in America.

Incidentally, the Mustang II notchback almost didn't make it. The one such proposal at the November executive showing, designed by DeLaRossa's troops and called "Anaheim," had not gone over well at previous consumer clinics. But Iacocca, suspecting that the researchers had missed something, decided to give it one last chance, at San Francisco in February 1972. This time, consumer reaction was positive, so it was decided to make a "trunked" version of the already-approved fastback, this with barely 16 months remaining before production startup. "It seems we go through that with every Mustang program," said Jack Telnack, who later replaced Bordinat as Ford design chief. "We always start with the fastback....Then we find out the surveys still say fifty-fifty [preference] and we have to add the notchback." Ford also investigated a two-seat fastback in February 1972 (via a full-scale tape drawing). It looked nice but was never seriously in contention.

Designing the Mustang II interior was far less involved. It was chiefly the work of L. David Ash, whose design credits included the mid-Fifties Crown Victoria,

roofline sketches and full-size tape drawings utilizing the approved fastback's lower body design. One of my sketch proposals was selected for development under my direction as a full-size clay model; this was followed by a finished fiberglass model at full size. I was asked to propose the clay version as a coupe with fixed side-window frames, and to have the fiberglass design made up as a true hardtop with frameless window edges.

As work on the coupe progressed, we ran into a potential sheetmetal-forming problem on the rear body corners. As conceived, several different surface planes and creased line breaks came together in a sharp point; the body engineering people believed the sheetmetal would split and tear during stamping operations. Their verdict was that the piece could not be produced as designed. Fortunately, one of the more adventurous body engineers was positive he had seen

that sort of formed section before, and asked me for suggestions. I remembered that the full-size '63 Chevys had a similarly shaped rear fender corner, so the engineer and I located just such a Chevy rear quarter panel at a local junkyard. When we displayed the old part—rust and all—for review in our studio, our point was made.

When completed, the fastback and notchback-coupe models were turned over to the Ford production studio for final detail work. It was at this stage that my coupe roofline was revised into a stiffer, more formal look.

Designing Mustang II continued: Variations

I created other coupe proposals, as well. One of them featured a "formal" quarter-

window shape with a thick, bright molding outline around the window's nearly vertical back edge. A variation of this idea was later used on the quarter-window treatment of the 1983-86 Thunderbird.

Another of my coupe themes was influenced by the recently introduced Mercedes-Benz 450 SLC four-place luxury coupe. I felt that the louvered quarter-window treatment imparted an elegant, semi-private character that would have worked well on the Mustang.

Our studio also was asked to do some proposals for a domestic Capri variation of the Mustang II, using the unchanged front fenders, doors, rear decklid, and both bumpers. I did a sketch proposal using a new rear quarter and taillight panel that featured such European Capri themes as the two simulated quarter intake scoops and the "flying buttress" roofline with a slightly

Renderings by designer Dick Nesbitt (*opposite page and this page bottom*) in late 1971-early 1972 show the Mustang II taking shape on a shorter 96.2-inch wheelbase. An early 1972 clay mock-up (*left*) shows the front end close to final form, but the side windows are not yet finalized, nor are the taillights on the January 24 study below it. Mrs. Anna Muccioli had complained at the '68 Ford annual stockholders meeting that the Mustang was getting too fat, so Henry Ford II showed her the smaller new Mustang II in 1973 (*below*). She approved.

inset backlight. This sketch went over very well; some Ford people favored it over the final Mustang II design.

My involvement with the Mustang II continued some time later, when I was assigned to the Pinto-Mustang-Maverick interior design studio. I arrived just in time to contribute to the development of a series of plush "Ghia"-level Mustang II interior themes.

Designing Mustang II continued: Looking Back

As I reflect on the styling development of the Mustang II, I'm disappointed that a project with such promise wound up as so much less than it could have been. Few will dispute that the "Mustang III" series that bowed in 1979 improved on the Mustang II in virtually all respects. Small wonder that Mustang's success continues to this day.

among others. Ash decided to give his interior mock-up the feel of a real automobile by making it much more realistic than is customary in the design business. It even had exterior sheetmetal and all four wheels attached. "It was a time-consuming thing to build," Ash said, "but it served its purpose very well. We didn't have to go through an elaborate series of meetings to determine everything. It was all approved right here. We were on a crash basis to get it done, and it was very enthusiastically received...."

Ash later confessed that his design was at least partly inspired by the likes of Jaguar, Rolls-Royce, and Mercedes. "We put everything in that we could conceive of that connotes restrained elegance, plus the get-up-and-go that says Mustang—something of a fire breather....It's a kind of a mini T-Bird."

Unlike the massive, heavily sculptured twin-cowl instrument panels of 1969-73,

The '74 Mustang II featured bucket seats and complete instrumentation (*above*). The notchback coupe is seen here in regular (*below*) and Ghia form (*opposite*). Lee Iacocca (*top*) had inspired the smaller '74 Mustang II.

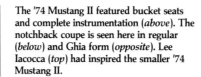

the Mustang II panel was dominated by a simple large oblong directly ahead of the driver. This put all controls close at hand, yet still had room for all necessary warning lights and instruments. Surprisingly, the latter included a standard tachometer, temperature gauge, and ammeter. Seats were initially covered in pleated cloth, vinyl, or optional leather—very plush. They had no rake adjustment, sad to say, but were definitely more comfortable than previous Mustang seats. Rear legroom

was limited, because the new car was seen as being used primarily by one or two adults, who'd sit in front. Back-seat room would be sufficient only for a couple of small children or for an adult passenger to be comfortable for a short time.

Dimensionally, the Mustang II retained the expected long-hood/short-deck proportions but on a reduced scale—smaller even than the original. The real target was sporty import coupes. The tape measure told the story:

Dimension (in.)	1965 Mustang	1974 Mustang II	1974 Toyota Celica
wheelbase	108.0	94.2	95.5
length	181.6	175.0	163.9
width	70.2	68.2	63.0
height	51.0	49.9	51.6

Against the '73 Mustang, the "II" was 20 inches shorter overall and nearly 13 inches in wheelbase, four inches narrower, an inch lower, and 400-500 pounds lighter.

At announcement time, some observers

suggested the Mustang II was just a sportier Pinto—which was more or less how it started, of course—and, sure enough, a good many components were shared. Even wheelbase was the same. But Pinto was actually upgraded for '74 to take advantage of some parts and features designed for the Mustang II.

For example, both models employed unit construction and the same front suspension—independent with unequal-length upper and lower arms and coil springs. For the Mustang, however, the lower arms were attached to a rubber-mounted subframe; on the Pinto they bolted directly to the main structure. By carrying the rear of the engine/transmission assembly, the sub-frame reduced driveline vibration to the Mustang II's passenger compartment. It also contributed to more precise steering and a smoother ride than Pinto's. Watchful company cost accountants could justify this more expensive mounting arrangement

A '74 Mustang II is being put through its paces on the test track (*opposite, bottom*). The fastback started at $3328 base (*left*) or as a Mach 1 (*top*) for $3674. The latter came with a 170-cid V-6 standard; it was rated at 105 horsepower. The base models had to make do with an 88-bhp 140-cid four. For 1975, the upmarket Ghia coupe adopted opera windows and a stand-up hood ornament (*opposite, top*). It sold for $3938.

179

because Mustang II was intended to sell for more than Pinto.

Both cars also used the same rack-and-pinion steering mechanism, but the Mustang's was mounted differently, again to minimize shock, and could be power-assisted at extra cost (Pinto's couldn't). At the rear, the Mustang's leaf springs were two inches longer than Pinto's, and its shock absorbers were staggered, as in previous high-performance Mustangs. Spring rates were computer-calculated to match equipment, weight, and body style of each car. The Ghia notchback, for example, came with very soft settings, while the optional competition suspension had the stiffest springs, along with a thicker front anti-roll bar, a rear bar, and Gabriel adjustable shock absorbers.

As mentioned, the eventual Mustang II concept gave no thought to a V-8, a first in Mustang history. Initial engine choices were limited to a 2.3-liter (140-cubic-inch) single-overhead-cam inline four and a 2.8-liter (171-cid) overhead-valve V-6.

Sometimes referred to as the "Lima" engine, because it was supplied from Ford's Lima, Ohio, plant, the four was the first American-built engine based on metric dimensions. That wasn't surprising. Originally designed for some of Ford's larger European cars, it was actually a bored-and-stroked version of the 2.0-liter Pinto unit. A novel feature was its "monolithic engine timing." After each engine was assembled, an electronic device hooked to a computer was connected to two engine sensors, an indicator point at the rear of the crankshaft and an electrical terminal between the distributor and coil. The computer compared readings from each sensor, then set timing automatically by means of a distributor adjustment. The computer's high degree of precision made this technique very useful for meeting increasingly tough emission standards.

The V-6 also had a European counterpart, and used the same camshaft, valvetrain, pushrods, and distributor. It was, in fact, the same engine available in U.S. Capris from 1972. However, it, too, was bored and stroked for Mustang II duty, with capacity increasing from 2.6 liters (155 cid) to 2.8. At the same time, Ford switched it from siamesed to separate exhaust ports for improved performance and thermal efficiency. Supplied only with dual exhausts, the V-6 was optional for

any Mustang II save the Mach 1 hatchback, where it was standard. Like early 2.0-liter Pinto fours, it was imported.

The Mustang II's standard four-speed gearbox was basically the four-speed unit from the British Ford Cortina as used in the Pinto, albeit strengthened to handle the Mustang's more powerful engines. Brakes were a combination of 9.3-inch front discs and 9 × 1.75-inch rear drums with vacuum assist.

Predictably, "cooking" Mustang IIs and the new top-line Ghia notchback (replacing Grandé as the luxury model) exhibited typically "American" ride and handling characteristics. The Mach 1 was both more capable and entertaining, with its standard

V-6, radial tires, and optional competition suspension. No Mustang II had overwhelming acceleration. The car was heavy for its size (curb weight was 2650-2900 pounds), so a V-6 with four-speed would do 0-60 mph in a lackluster 13-14 seconds and reach only about 100 mph, a far cry from the big-block V-8 days. As if to prepare buyers for this reduced performance, Ford redesigned the trademark running-horse emblem for the Mustang II, a less muscular steed that seemed to be trotting instead of galloping.

Mustang II didn't change significantly during its five-year production life. The four-cylinder and V-6 Ghia as well as the V-6-only Mach 1 were available for the

full run, and Ford continued to provide a lengthy list of options for all models. Aside from air conditioning and a variety of radios and tape players, the 1974 roster included a vinyl top, and sunroof, among other items.

Options expanded for 1975 to include a $454 flip-up glass "moonroof" for the already posh Ghia, as well as a new Silver Luxury Package with cranberry-color crushed-velour upholstery, silver paint and vinyl top, and depressingly, a standup hood ornament. At the same time, the rear-quarter glass on all Ghias was shortened up to form "opera" windows, a popular styling fad of the day.

Other new '75 options included forged aluminum wheels and an extended-range (17-gallon) fuel tank. The latter betrayed the fact that even the smallest of Fords were rather thirsty in this period, but mid-model year brought partial relief in a special "MPG" notchback and fastback with that new emissions cleanup device, the catalytic converter. This obviated the need for much add-on emissions hardware and allowed engine retuning to improve fuel efficiency. The MPGs vanished after this short run, but the "cat con," of course, would live on.

But the big news for '75 was the return of the small-block V-8, Ford's answer to the pleas of the small but enthusiastic band of buyers who still craved performance—emissions and safety requirements not-

withstanding. Offered optionally through '78, this was, of course, the familiar 302-cid unit, tuned to deliver 122 net horsepower, increased to 139 bhp for '76. Cooling requirements dictated larger grille egg-crates, a change applied to all models regardless of engine after 1974.

Since the Mustang V-8 displaced about 5.0 liters and Chevrolet's Monza 2+2 (based on its subcompact Vega rival to Pinto) offered a 4.3-liter (262-cid) V-8, comparisons were inevitable. The editors of *Road & Track* clearly preferred the Monza. And, despite the subjective judgments involved, they were probably right. Monza was brand-new for '75, a fresh, modern design that seemed smoother and

Ford showed a T-top version of the Mustang
II at some 1976 auto shows. It sported a
thick band that went over the roof. Favorable
public reaction inspired Ford to bring out a
production model in 1977.

more integrated than the Mustang II. And its comfort, ride, handling, and fuel economy were all judged to be better than the Ford's. *R&T* summed up the feelings of many in saying the Mustang II's styling was "humpy and bumpy, and—in its interior—downright garish" and lacking "ergonomic refinement." Mustang beat the Monza for acceleration by a healthy margin, as one would expect with more displacement, but it also used more gas. The Ford's only advantage seemed to be in braking. Here are *R&T*'s test results:

	Mustang II	Monza 2+2
V-8 cid/bhp/rpm	302/122/ 3600	262/110/ 3600
0-to-60 mph, sec.	10.5	13.4
¼-mile, speed/sec.	77.0/17.9	72.5/19.5
top speed, mph	106	103
fuel economy, mpg	13.0	17.0

Overall Mustang II sales were down over 50 percent for 1975, but would hold steady at about 190,000 a year through the end of the line in 1978. If not exactly torrid, this was certainly a lot more encouraging—not to mention profitable— than the tepid 1971-73 pace.

In further pursuit of sport—or what was left of it—Ford offered a "boy racer" Mustang II for 1976. Called Cobra II, it was basically a trim option (initially priced at $312) in the image of the late, great Shelby-Mustangs. Available only on three-doors, it comprised sports steering wheel, remote-control door mirrors, and brushed-aluminum appliqués on dash and door panels, plus a black grille, styled steel wheels with trim rings, radial tires, flip-out rear quarter windows with louvered covers, front air dam, rear spoiler, and simulated hood air scoop. Requisite model ID and/or badges appeared on rocker panels, grille, tail, and front fenders. The '76s were all done in white with blue tape stripes (applied to rockers, hood, rooftop, and tail), but other combinations were added beginning with the '77s. It was flashy, but a far cry from the Shelby-Mustangs it tried to emulate. Incidentally, the package could be ordered on the Mach 1, which created the amusing official designation Mustang II Mach 1 Cobra II.

No less subtle was the Stallion, another all-show/no-go trim option that was also offered (in slightly different form) on '76 Pintos and Mavericks. Again restricted to Mustang II fastbacks, it included silver body sides and black elsewhere, plus forged-aluminum wheels, all set off by

snorting horse-head front-fender decals. One other change involved the Ghia moon-roof, which was now optional for any Mustang II notchback and available with either silver or brown tint.

For 1977 came a special new Ghia option, the "Sports Appearance Group,"

This page: The 1976 Stallion option (*top and center*) was strictly for show. Note the headlight treatment on this 1978 Mustang II show car (*bottom*). *Opposite page*: The 1976 Mustang IIs, even with their various trim options, could hardly be told from the 1974-75 models.

offered only with black or tan paint. This included many color-keyed components, including console, three-spoke sports steering wheel, cast aluminum wheels with chamois-color spokes, and a trunk luggage rack with hold-down straps and bright buckles. Wheel choices expanded to include "lacy spoke" aluminum rims in chrome or with white-painted spokes and red trim rings. A new T-top roof with twin lift-off glass panels arrived for fastbacks only. Replacing the Stallion option was a Rallye Appearance Package comprising black

paint with subtle gold accents, and two-toning became optional on most Mustang IIs for the first time.

Still available (at $160-$400 depending on model) was the useful Rallye Package for all but four-cylinder models. This grouped the competition suspension with Traction-Lok limited-slip differential, an "extra-cooling package," and dual exhausts with chrome tips. You also got larger raised-white-letter tires, color-keyed remote-adjustable door mirrors, leather-rim steering wheel and quartz digital clock.

Opposite page: The $599 Cobra II option on the '76 fastback was mainly a trim package sporting rocker panel racing stripes plus two wide stripes over the hood, roof, and rear deck. Other touches included a black grille with Cobra emblem, louvered rear quarter windows, styled steel wheels, front air dam, ducktail rear spoiler, fake hood scoop, and—of course—snake decals. With optional V-8, four-speed manual, and Rallye suspension, the Cobra II handled well and did 0-60 mph in nine seconds. The '77s (*this page*) looked the same.

This brings up the fact that though the Mustang II was a smaller and less potent ponycar, it hewed to Mustang tradition in its long list of options, both packages and individual items. Among those not already mentioned: anti-theft alarm system (about $75), electric rear-window defroster ($60-$75), flip-out rear-quarter windows for fastbacks ($30), fold-down rear seat for notchbacks (around $60; standard on fastbacks), center console ($65), several sound systems (including a new AM/FM radio with cassette player), and the usual power assists. The competition suspension added only $25-$60 depending on model and year.

For 1978, Ford again tried "paint-on performance" with the King Cobra option. Like the Cobra II, which continued, this ensemble was available only for the fastback, and had every racy styling touch any kid could want. There was a snake decal on the hood and tape stripes on the roof, rear deck, and rocker panels, around the wheel wells, and on the front air dam that was also included. "King Cobra" was writ large on each door, the air dam, and on the standard decklid spoiler. A black-finish grille, window

moldings, headlamp bezels, and wiper arms plus a brushed-aluminum instrument panel appliqué completed the cosmetics. You also got the 302 V-8, power steering, the aforementioned Rallye Package, and Goodrich 70-series T/A radial tires. Given

A 1977 Stallion package was designed, but never saw production (*above*). The Mach 1 (*below*) could be ordered with V-8 and T-top. The Cobra II package was revised in late 1977, seen here on a '78 (*opposite, top*). The '78 Ghia was little changed.

Ford called the 1978 Mustang II King Cobra
"The new King of the Road!" And indeed
it was the ultimate Mustang II; aside from
the wild, bespoilered styling, it all had the
performance and handling goodies. An
estimated 500 were built.

all that bold advertising, this was the least Ford could do, and it's probably true that the King Cobra's 17-second quarter-mile time was high performance by 1978 standards.

Also new for '78 were an electronic voltage regulator, variable-ratio gearing for the optional power steering (replacing fixed-ratio), "Wilshire" cloth seating for the Ghia, and a Fashion Accessory Package for the standard notchback. The last comprised door pockets, striped fabric upholstery, lighted vanity mirror, and four-way manual driver's seat, all clearly aimed at women buyers. Fortunately, such chauvinistic appeals were on the way out.

Otherwise, the '78s were much like earlier Mustang IIs. Sales were still holding up: 192,000 for the model year, second only to introductory 1974. They might have been higher, but some '78s were

The 1978 Mustang II Ghia listed at $4149. Ford said it "combines tasteful elegance with a beautiful driving experience," and with the optional 302 V-8 (*left*) it offered sprightly get-up-and-go. Of the 192,410 Mustang IIs built in 1978, 34,730 wore a Ghia badge.

1974-78 MUSTANG AT A GLANCE

Model Year Production

No.	Model	1974	1975	1976	1977*	1978
60F	2-dr. cpe.	177,671	85,155	78,508	67,783	81,304
60H	Ghia 2-dr. cpe.	89,477	52,320	37,515	29,510	34,730
69F	3-dr. cpe.	74,799	30,038	62,312	49,161	68,408
69R	Mach 1 3-dr. cpe.	44,046	21,062	9,232	6,719	7,968
	TOTAL	385,993	188,575	187,567	153,173	192,410

*Includes vehicles produced as 1978 models but sold as 1977 models.

Prices/Weights
($/lbs)

No.	Model	1974	1975	1976	1977	1978
02	2-dr. I-4	$3134/2620	$3529/2660	$3525/2678	$3702/2627	$3731/2608
03	3-dr. I-4	$3328/2699	$3818/2697	$3781/2706	$3901/2672	$3975/2654
04	Ghia 2-dr. I-4	$3480/2886	$3938/2704	$3859/2729	$4119/2667	$4149/2646
02	2-dr. V-6	$3363/2689	$3801/2775	$3791/2756	$3984/2750	$3944/2705
03	3-dr. V-8	$3557/2768	$4090/2812	$4047/2784	$4183/2975	$4188/2751
04	Ghia 2-dr. V-6	$3709/2755	$4210/2819	$4125/2807	$4401/2790	$4362/2743
05	Mach 1, V-6	$3674/2778	$4188/2879	$4209/2822	$4332/2785	$4430/2733

General Specifications

	1974	1975	1976	1977	1978
Wheelbase (in.)	96.2	96.2	96.2	96.2	96.2
Overall length (in.)	175.0	175.0	175.0	175.0	175.0
Overall width (in.)	70.2	70.2	70.2	70.2	70.2
Std. Trans.	4-sp. man.	4-sp. man.	4-sp. man.	4-sp. man.	4-sp. man.
Optional Trans.	3-sp. auto.	3-sp. auto.	3-sp. auto.	3-sp. auto.	3-sp. auto.

Engine Availability

Type	cid	bhp	1974	1975	1976	1977	1978
I-4	140	a	Std.	Std.	Std.	Std.	Std.
V-6	171	b	Opt.[d]	Opt.[d]	Opt.[d]	Opt.[d]	Opt.[d]
V-8	302	c	—	Opt.	Opt.	Opt.	Opt.

a: rated 85 bhp 1974; 83 bhp 1975; 92 bhp 1976; 89 bhp 1977; 88 bhp 1978
b: rated 105 bhp 1974; 97 bhp 1975; 103 bhp 1976; 93 bhp 1977; 90 bhp 1978
c: rated 122 bhp 1975; 139 bhp 1976-78
d: standard Mach 1

delivered to dealers earlier than usual and registered as '77s, due to low inventory.

Yet despite its popularity when new, the Mustang II has few fans today. Its styling has not aged gracefully and, for enthusiasts, its "less ponycar" character is a depressing reminder of the trials and tribulations that made the mid-Seventies such a dull period for all Detroit cars.

In retrospect, however, the Mustang II has significance in bridging the gap between the last of the traditional Mustangs and the first of an exciting new generation of Ford ponycars for an age that would prove even more difficult. That's no small task for any car, and few have done it better. We can thus be grateful for the Mustang II. You may not like it, but it kept the ponycar spirit alive in Dearborn, and for that it deserves our respect.

Ford built a total of 1,107,718 Mustang IIs during its five-year run. Collectors tend to shun them, as they do most mid-Seventies cars, but over time some of the more desirable models should attract at least a minor following. In fact, the '78 King Cobra (*left*) is already being collected—but try to find one!

CHAPTER EIGHT

1979-81:
A
Legend
Reborn

Although a modest sales winner, the Mustang II never inspired the same enthusiasm as earlier Mustangs. But another revolution was underway in Dearborn, and it culminated in the all-new Ford ponycar that bowed (without a Roman numeral suffix) for 1979.

Clean and taut, crisp yet substantial-looking, this fifth-generation Mustang combined the best thinking of American and European design: deft surface execution, a simple downswept nose, ample glass area, and a pleasing lack of ornamentation. Those who got close enough to see the

familiar running horse (which now looked more like its original self) must have been impressed. At long last, Ford had created the kind of restrained, efficient, elegant sporty car it set out to build in the first place.

Of course, the '79 inherited some

perennial Mustang problems. Handling remained far from perfect, the driving position too low and interior space limited. And workmanship wasn't as solid or thorough as on European and Japanese competitors like the Volkswagen Scirocco and Toyota Celica. But no car can be faultless, especially one selling at such a comparatively low price. By almost any standard, the '79 Mustang was a most attractive buy.

Like Mustang II and the original Mustang, the '79's final shape was selected from proposals submitted by competing

Opposite page: Work began on a successor to the Mustang II almost as soon as it debuted. An early study (*top*) borrowed much of its basic shape from the Mustang II fastback. Some styling ideas from 1975 (*bottom and this page*) looked closer to what emerged as the 1980 Thunderbird.

199

in-house teams: this time the Ford and Lincoln-Mercury production studios, Advanced Design, and Ford's Ghia operation in Italy (by this time under Don DeLaRossa). All were given the same design parameters (the so-called "hard points" that include length, width, wheelbase, cowl height, etc.) from which they developed sketches, clay models, and fiberglass mockups. Quarter-scale clay models were tested for 136 hours in wind tunnels. Reason: aerodynamics was being increasingly recognized (rediscovered actually, from the lessons of streamlining in the Thirties) as important to improved fuel economy, a new fact of life in the aftermath of the 1973-74 energy crisis.

Washington's heavy hand had already been felt anew in something called CAFE, short for "corporate average fuel economy." The result of post-energy-crisis legislation, it mandated specific mpg targets for all cars sold by all automakers doing business in the U.S., effective with model year 1978. In brief, CAFE required that the EPA-rated fuel economy of all cars sold by a given company average so many miles per gallon for a given year—initially 19 mpg, rising progressively to 27.5 mpg by 1985. Companies whose "fleet average" fell below the specified targets would be fined a set number of dollars for each 0.1 mpg deviation—multiplied by total sales for that model year. Obviously, failure to comply could be costly indeed. However, the law also provided credits to those manufacturers exceeding a given year's target that could be either carried forward or carried back to avoid or reduce penalties for non-compliance in another year.

It was all highly political, of course, not to mention controversial and more than a little complicated. Nevertheless, CAFE achieved its intended effect of spurring Detroit to develop smaller, lighter, thriftier cars in most every size/price category—

Ford stylists spent considerable time on "formal" themes for the '79 Mustang design. By the fall of 1975 there were a number of ideas being tried (*both pages*), initially with the "7-X Maverick" working title, but based on the "Fox" platform to be used by the 1978 Fairmont. Stylists were working in early 1976 (*opposite, bottom*) around a 105.1-inch wheelbase, very close to the 100.4-inch wheelbase that the production 1979 Mustang utilized.

As with the Mustang II, the 1979 Mustang
bowed in two body styles: fastback and,
here, the notchback.

really a continuation of the "downsizing" trend begun by General Motors with its full-size 1977 models. Adding new urgency to this effort was the onset of another energy crisis in 1979, triggered when the Shah of Iran was deposed in favor of an America-hating Ayatollah who cut off the country's oil exports and went to war with Iraq. But the ensuing oil shortage soon became an oil glut, and this, plus a turnaround in the U.S. economy and the Reagan Administration's more relaxed attitude toward legislated restrictions on business, would render CAFE all but meaningless by the mid-Eighties.

Detroit was still reeling from the first energy crisis when work began on a successor to the Mustang II in mid-1975. The design brief called for using the basic suspension and floorpan of the evolving "Fox" project, which had been initiated in early 1973 to develop "a new corporate worldwide sport/family/four/five-passenger sedan." In America, Fox was originally

204

slated to replace both Mustang II and the subcompact Pinto, but it ended up a compact, the Ford Fairmont/Mercury Zephyr twins that took over from the 1970-vintage Maverick/Comet for 1978.

Ford planners said the Fox platform could be shortened somewhat for the new Mustang, and it ultimately was: by 5.1 inches in wheelbase, to 100.4 inches. Mustang II power units—2.3-liter four, 2.8-liter V-6 and 302 V-8—would be retained. As with the original ponycar, curb weight was pegged at a comparatively low 2700 pounds. The interior would be larger than the Mustang II's, but still mainly designed to seat two adults comfortably, four in a pinch.

Like the original Mustang but unlike the II, the notchback model was styled first and the fastback developed from it. Of the finished, full-size fiberglass models shown to top management, the one chosen as the basis for production styling came from a team headed by Jack Telnack, then execu-

Ford designers were kept quite busy working on the '79 Mustang in 1976 (*both pages*). A February study (*opposite, top left*) clearly showed its relationship with the upcoming Fairmont/Zephyr; next to it is a proposed two-seater. Two other mock-ups (*bottom row*) sported a rear side window treatment much like the Fairmont Futura coupe.

The 1979 Mustang hid its Fairmont-based
heritage far better than some of the early
styling studies did.

tive director of Ford North American Light Truck and Car Design. Telnack had just returned from Ford Europe, where he'd spearheaded prototype development for the pretty front-drive Fiesta minicar (sold stateside in 1978-80). Four trim levels would initially be offered: standard, Sport Option, Ghia, and Cobra. The last arrived with black-finish greenhouse trim and lower bodysides, color-keyed body moldings, and an optional snake decal for the hood, plus sportier seats and cabin appointments.

Telnack described the fifth-generation design effort in June 1978: "One of the basic themes for this car was 'form follows function'....We wanted to be as aerodynamically correct as possible before getting into the wind tunnel. In the past we have designed cars and then gone into the tunnel mainly for tuning the major surfaces that have been approved....With the Mustang, the designers were thinking about aerodynamics in the initial sketch stages, which made the tuning job in the tunnel much easier. Consequently, we wound up with the most slippery car ever done in the Ford Motor Company: a drag coefficient of 0.44 for the three-door fastback, 0.46 for the two-door notchback. [Aerodynamics is] probably the most cost-effective way to improve corporate average fuel economy. We know that a 10-percent [reduction] in drag can result in a five-percent improvement in fuel economy at a steady-state 50 mph....That's really worthwhile stuff for us to go after."

It should be noted that though the drag figures Telnack quoted were good for '78, they'd soon be mediocre. Ford's 1983 Thunderbird, for example, arrived at an altogether more impressive 0.35. While that difference may not seem dramatic, it represents a reduction of over 20 percent, and shows just how radically standards can change in a few years.

Fritz Mayhew did a series of sketches in 1977 that expressed the spirit of the 1979 Mustang (*both pages*). They took liberties in interpreting the Mustang theme, but the basic design of the '79 production model can be seen clearly in these drawings, notably in the front end design, the fluting behind the rear side windows, and the wraparound taillights. Of course, the '79 design was locked up by this time.

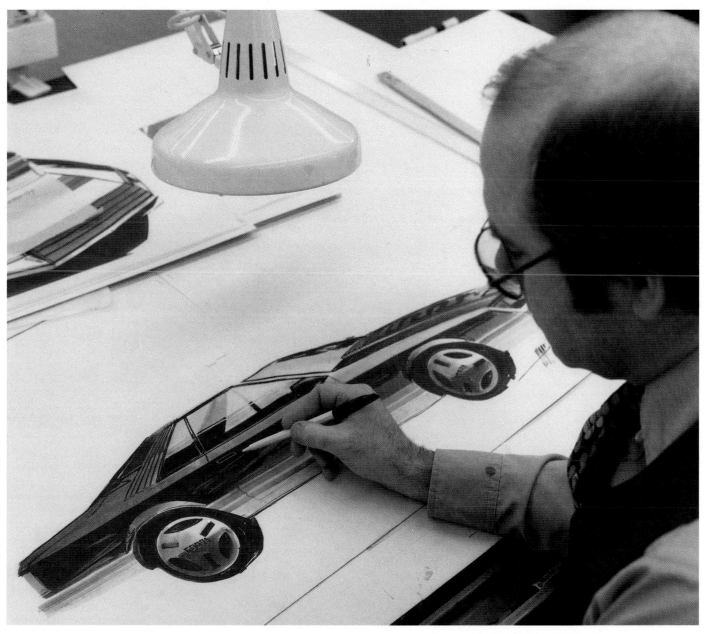

Key members of Telnack's team included Light Car Design Manager Fritz Mayhew, pre-production design executive David Rees, and pre-production designer Gary Haas. The shape they evolved was a sort of notchback wedge: very slim up front, with the hood sloped down from a rather high cowl—actually an inch higher than Fairmont/Zephyr's. Telnack said this was to "get a faster sloping hood...to pivot the hood over the air cleaner." This dictated special inner front fender aprons and radiator supports instead of Fairmont/Zephyr pieces, but everyone agreed the extra expense was warranted. Increased fuel economy was one reward. Another was racier appearance, as expected in a Mustang. Aerodynamic considerations

also prompted a slight lip on the decklid and a small spoiler integrated with the front bumper. A distinctive touch was black-finish vertical slats behind the rear side windows, rather like those of the Mercedes 450SLC. They hindered over-the-shoulder vision, however, one of the new design's less functional aspects.

Body engineering aimed at holding the line on weight in the interest of both fuel economy and performance, which implied maximum use of lightweight materials.

The 5.0 badge on the front fender of this '79 Mustang means that it has the 302-cid, 140-bhp V-8. Also offered were a 2.3-liter, 88-bhp four, a turbo version with 140 bhp, a 170-cid V-6 with 109 bhp, and—later in the year—a 200-cid, 91-bhp inline six.

Sure enough, plastics, aluminum, and high-strength/low-alloy (HSLA) steel all figured prominently. A significant new plastics technology appeared in color-keyed bumper covers of soft urethane made by the reaction-injection molding (RIM) process. HSLA steel was used for rear suspension arms and the number-three frame cross-member, while aluminum was found in drivetrains and in the bumpers of some models. Thinner but stronger glass saved additional pounds, as did slimmer-section doors. As a result, the 1979 Mustang was some 200 pounds lighter on average than Mustang II despite being slightly larger in every dimension. In an age of downsizing, this was a notable achievement.

Interior design received equally careful attention. Total volume rose by 14 cubic feet on the notchback and by 16 cubic feet on the hatchback. The thinner doors

opened up 3.6 inches more shoulder room and 2.0 inches more hiproom in front. Back-seat gains measured 5.0 and 6.0 inches, respectively. Rear legroom expanded by over five inches. Cargo volume enlarged by two cubic feet on the notchback and four on the hatchback.

Reflecting Telnack's European experience were standard full instrumentation (speedometer, trip odometer, tachometer, temperature gauge, oil pressure gauge, ammeter, and fuel gauge) and new fingertip stalks for turn signals/headlight dimmer/ horn and wiper/washer (shared with

The '79 Mustang evolves (*opposite, top*). It was the first Mustang designed with aerodynamics in mind, and was subjected to intensive wind tunnel evaluation (*top right*). The final design chosen (*opposite, bottom*) was the work of a team headed by Jack Telnack (*above, man in center*).

Fairmont/Zephyr, as was the basic instrument panel and cowl structure). A third lever (on the right) was provided when the extra-cost tilt steering wheel was ordered.

Practical new convenience options ran to interval-sweep wipers and a console complete with a graphic display for "vehicle systems monitoring." The latter was a profile outline of the car on which warning lights were placed to indicate low fuel, low windshield washer fluid, and failed headlights, taillights, or brake lamps. A push-button allowed the driver to check that the display itself was okay. The console also housed a quartz-crystal digital chronometer that showed time, date, or elapsed time at the touch of a button. Finally, luxury-trim models were given higher-quality materials, and the '79 Ghia was far less flashy than its '78 counterpart.

Like past Mustangs, the '79 was designed for the broadest possible market appeal. Said Ford Division marketing plans manager Michael Woods: "Not too long ago

we did a concept study on positioning the [imported] Capri and brought in imported-car owners, some Capri owners—people who own small specialty cars. We showed them the [new Mustang] and talked to them about strategy. We were pretty gratified that an awful lot of people who were interested in the [imported] Capri felt

that we had maintained the Capri theme—the functional styling of the car—and that it was consistent with the original car."

Now the European Capri, especially with V-6, was a very competent touring car. For the new Mustang to match it, specifications would have to be greatly altered. Capri fans would not be satisfied with a plush,

As in the past, the Mustang could be ordered with a Cobra package in 1979. The car shown here features a special suspension with Michelin 190/65R390 TRX tires and forged aluminum wheels, not to mention the most intriguing engine option in 1979, a 2.3-liter turbo four. It cranked out 140 bhp and went from 0-55 in 8.3 seconds.

short-wheelbase coupe that weighed too much and handled sluggishly. At the same time, Ford didn't want to lose all those thousands of Mustang II buyers. Several levels of suspension capability were thus deemed necessary.

As planned, the basic hardware was Fairmont/Zephyr. The front suspension employed modified MacPherson-strut geometry instead of conventional upper A-arms. Unlike similar setups still found in many European and most Japanese cars, the coil spring did not wrap around the strut but mounted between a lower control arm and the body structure, which eliminated the need for an expensive spring compressor for replacing shocks. A front anti-roll bar was specified for all models, with diameter varied according to engine.

Rear geometry employed a four-bar link arrangement, also with coil springs —lighter and more compact than the Mustang II's leaf-spring Hotchkiss setup. V-8 models would have a standard rear anti-roll bar. Since this served more for lateral location than controlling sway, the car's roll center was effectively lowered

and rear spring rates could be commensurately softer.

Product planners ultimately decided to offer three suspension levels—standard, "handling," and "special"—each designed for and issued with its own set of tires. The basic setup was tuned for conventional bias-plys, the mid-level package for regular radials. The special suspension was designed around Michelin's recently developed TRX radials, whose unusual 390-mm (15.35-inch) diameter required matching forged-aluminum wheels.

Initially available only with 14-inch radials, the handling package upgraded the basic chassis with higher spring rates, different shock valving, and stiffer bushings. A rear stabilizer bar was also provided

Prices of the '79 Mustang started at $4494 for a four-cylinder two-door coupe, $4828 for the hatchback. Ghia models listed at $5064 and $5216, respectively. Although the new Mustang was bigger in almost every dimension and rode a four-inch-longer wheelbase, weight was actually reduced a bit. The public took to the '79 by driving home 332,025 units, smartly up on 1978 results.

when the 2.8-liter V-6 was ordered. The special suspension provided even better handling; company press releases boasted that it was engineered "to extract maximum performance" from the 190/65R-390 Michelin tires. (Ford already had experience with this wheel/tire combination, on its European Granada.) This meant specific shock-absorber valving, high-rate rear springs, 1.12-inch front stabilizer bar, and a rear bar.

There was no need to change the Mustang II's precise rack-and-pinion steering. Power assist was still optional, and the variable-ratio rack issued for 1978 also returned. Again to save weight, housings for both the manual and power systems were constructed of die-cast aluminum.

Besides Mustang II engines, the '79 was offered with an intriguing new powerplant: a turbocharged version of the standard 2.3-liter "Lima" four, with a rated 131 SAE net horsepower against only 88 bhp for the unblown unit. Though they're common now, turbos were pretty exotic at the time, let alone on a mass-market American car. With four-speed gearbox, the blown four was good for a claimed 8.3 seconds in 0-55-mph acceleration (with the "double nickel" national speed limit in force, Detroit wasn't quoting 0-60 times), plus fuel economy in the mid-20s.

Though turbocharging was new to Mustang, it had been around for years—like the similar supercharging method, a bolt-on means of improving volumetric efficiency. The principle is simple. A turbine located in the flow of exhaust gases is connected to an impeller (compressor) near the carburetor. In normal running, the turbine spins too slowly to boost manifold pressure or affect fuel consumption. As the throttle is opened, however, the engine speeds up, which increases the flow of exhaust gases. The increased flow spins the turbine, which speeds up the impeller and increases the density (pressure) of the air/fuel mixture fed to the combustion chambers. The result: more power. To prevent engine damage, maximum boost was limited to six pounds per square inch by a relief valve that allowed gases to bypass the turbine once that pressure was reached.

Carryover engines weren't neglected. The venerable 302 V-8 a no-charge alternative

to the turbo-four with the Cobra option gained a new low-restriction exhaust system, more light-weight components, and a ribbed V-belt for the accessory drive. The German-made V-6 was in short supply, so the old 200-cubic-inch inline six was

brought back to replace it late in the model year. The V-8 and both sixes could be teamed with an optional four-speed gearbox developed specifically for them—basically the standard three-speed manual with direct-drive third gear (1.0:1 ratio)

and an overdrive gear (0.70:1) tacked on. Final drive ratios were 3.08:1 for automatics, four-speed V-6, and the unblown four-cylinder engine, 3.45:1 for all other drivetrain combinations. The automatic, by the way, was the familiar three-speed

Cruise-O-Matic as used in the Mustang II.

Per Mustang tradition, the performance of any particular '79 depended on drivetrain. The V-8 was a drag-race engine by late-Seventies standards: 0-60 mph clocked out at about nine seconds. With four-speed,

The 1980 Mustang, in the sophomore year of its design cycle, was predictably little changed. The turbo four, as on the car above, still belted out 140 horsepower, but the optional V-8 was now a 255-cid unit rated at a meager 117 horses.

the V-6 was still in the 13-14-second range, while a like-equipped turbo-four did the trip in about 12-12.5 seconds.

As expected, press reaction also varied with powertrain. Some writers thought the V-8 Mustang was overpowered and out of step with gasoline prices that were on the rise again. Predictably, the intriguing turbo-four garnered the most "buff book" attention. Said *Road & Track*'s John Dinkel: "The TRX turbo would seem to be an enthusiast's delight. I just hope that the design compromises dictated by costs and the fact that Ford couldn't start with a completely clean sheet of paper don't wreck that dream....There's no doubt the new Mustang has the potential to be the best sport coupe Ford has ever built, but in some respects [it] is as enigmatic as its predecessor."

There was one more enigma brewing. A month after the press previewed the '79 Mustang, in June 1978, Lee Iacocca was fired as Ford Motor Company president. Officially, he was taking early retirement (on October 15, his 54th birthday). But many insiders had surmised that he'd be

dumped sometime before Henry Ford II was scheduled to retire as chief executive in 1980 and as chairman in 1982. As usual, the boss himself didn't say much, though he reportedly told Iacocca, "It's just one of those things." In removing a strong president, HFII was following a 50-year Ford tradition. Past presidents Bill Knudsen, Ernie Breech, and Bunkie

Knudsen had all been abruptly removed by him or his grandfather.

Iacocca wasn't bitter, at least publicly. Later he said, "You just surmise that the Breeches of the world got too big, too soon, and he [Ford] doesn't want strong guys around. You know, he wants to diffuse and bureaucratize the company as he gets to be 61. I guess that's the only thing I can

Top row: The Cobra epitomized the street Mustangs, promising hot performance even if it couldn't always back it up. No matter, Mustang served as the Indy 500 Pace Car (*opposite, bottom*) in 1979, and Ford grabbed the opportunity to build about 11,000 replicas. Ford also campaigned an IMSA racer in 1981 (its modified 1.7-liter four developed 560 bhp); it won at Brainerd and Sears Point.

come up with, because I really don't have a good sound answer myself."

Ironically, and as Iacocca carefully noted, June 1978 had been the biggest single sales month in Ford history, capping a first half that netted the company its largest six-month profit on record. "They probably won't be at this peak again," Iacocca said, "so I guess it's a good time to go."

Thus, after 32 years with Ford, Iacocca was a surprising free agent—though not for long, of course. He was too young, too vigorous to retire, and he yearned for a new challenge. He found it soon enough: at Chrysler Corporation, where he signed on as president, then as chairman, vowing to pull the industry's perennial number-three out of the financial quagmire in which it had been bogged down for too long.

Iacocca's appointment pleased a great many people, especially worried Chrysler

222

stockholders. Observed *Automotive News*: "Any other auto company would be willing to give up three future draft choices to get its hands on that kind of talent." Iacocca, said the editorial, "is a manager, a really professional manager. And he was paid a lot for his services...compensation that

reached a million dollars a year, figures that defy understanding by mere mortals. Yet by all standards, he earned every penny....The job he has done seems to speak for itself."

Back in Dearborn, Ford was readying a smaller-bore 255-cid V-8 to replace the

The 1980 Cobra package sported a revised grille, new hood scoop, and revised side graphics. Notice the Cobra logo in the rear side window. The second Arab oil embargo struck in 1979, pushing the industry into a sales slump that would get worse; Mustang output fell to 241,064 units.

302 option for the 1980 Mustang. The latest in a long line of Ford small-blocks dating from the original Fairlane 221 of 1962, it seemed an amazingly fast response to "Energy Crisis II" but was really prompted by CAFE and had thus been planned long before. Regardless, it was a definite help, though performance naturally suffered.

Styling changed only in detail. Nobody at Ford was unhappy with the latest Mustang's looks. Neither were customers.

In fact, because the market was strong for most of '79 and Ford's ponycar all-new, Mustang had scored a substantial sales gain over 1978, reaching just over 332,000 units. But the new Middle East turmoil devastated the 1980 market, and Mustang

suffered as much as any Detroit car. Though it remained seventh among domestic models, volume plunged to 241,000.

Mustang had been chosen for pace-car duty at the 1979 Indianapolis 500, so it was natural that an "Indy Pace Car" replica would appear as a mid-year addition to the line. It did, and went on to inspire the 1980 Cobra package, which gained a similar slat grille, plus more prominent

front and rear spoilers, integral foglamps, non-functioning hood scoop, and the special TRX suspension. Still built around the turbo-four and offered for the hatchback only, this package upped sticker price by $1482 (versus $1173 in '79). As before, the hood snake decal was a separate option ($88 this year, up $10).

Elsewhere, high-back, all-vinyl bucket seats and color-keyed interior and door

trim became across-the-board standards, as did more efficient halogen headlights (replacing conventional tungsten sealed-beams). Hatchbacks now came with the Sport Option at no charge, which meant styled sport wheels with trim rings, black rocker panel and window moldings, wide bodyside moldings, striped rub strip

extensions, and a sporty steering wheel.

The two Ghia models remained the luxury Mustangs for 1980, boasting color-keyed seatbelts, mirrors, bodyside moldings, and, on hatchbacks, C-pillar trim, plus low-back vinyl bucket seats with headrests, door map pockets, a visor vanity mirror, thicker pile carpeting, deluxe steer-

ing wheel, roof-mounted assist handles, and a full complement of interior lights. Leather or cloth-and-vinyl upholstery was available in six different colors.

Options were more numerous than ever. A partial list: tilt steering wheel, speed control, power door locks, remote trunklid or hatchback release, rear window wiper/

washer, flip-up glass sunroof, and a wide assortment of wheels, wheel covers, and audio systems. New to the slate were Recaro reclining front bucket seats, first offered on the '79 Pace Car Replica. With their infinitely variable seatback recliners and adjustable thigh and lumbar supports, Mustang could no longer be accused of

lagging behind its European competition in seat comfort.

Other new 1980 options included a roof-mounted luggage carrier, "window shade" cargo-area cover for the hatchback, and accent side tape stripes. An interesting dress-up item for notchbacks was the extra-cost Carriage Roof, a diamond-grain full vinyl covering set off by black window frames and moldings, designed to simulate the top-up appearance of a true convertible.

Save the smaller V-8, Mustang's 1980 drivetrain chart was essentially a photo-copy of late 1979's. Both fours still teamed with conventional four-speed manual transmission as standard. The six, still rated at modest 85 bhp (versus 109 for the now-departed V-6), came with the manual four-speed overdrive unit. Cruise-O-Matic was now your only choice with V-8 (Detroit was still playing games with "mandatory options") and extra-cost elsewhere.

Though an old-timer by 1980, that straight six was an efficient, easy-to-service engine. It had less horsepower than the superseded V-6, but this was offset by its greater displacement and torque, so "real-world" performance wasn't all that different. There was nothing exotic about it: seven-main-bearing crankshaft, hydraulic valve lifters, cast-iron block, one-barrel carburetor. But according to Ford's "Cost-of-Ownership" formula, where required maintenance for the first 50,000 miles is averaged according to dealer parts and labor prices, the inline six cost less to operate than the V-6, an important plus for inflation-weary buyers.

Mustang had been with us for 15 years by 1980, and it was natural to ask how the latest version compared with the '65 original. Judging by certain "vital statistics," it was tempting to say little had changed:

	1965 Mustang	1980 Mustang
Length (in.)	181.6	179.1
Width (in.)	68.2	69.1
Wheelbase (in.)	108.0	100.4
Weight, 6-cyl. (lb.)	2,445	2,516
base six, cid	200	200
base V-8, cid	260	255

Despite their similarity in numbers, these were really quite different Mustangs. Though the '80 was about as long as the '65 and had the same amount of front passenger room, it offered more rear-seat space despite a 7.6-inch shorter wheelbase. Ford had obviously learned something

about space utilization in 15 years. And though the '80 was burdened with all manner of government-mandated safety features such as reinforced doors and five-mph bumpers, it weighed hardly more than a comparable '65. Apparently, Ford had also learned something about lightweight materials and construction.

There were some equally interesting comparisons in the engine department. The 2.3-liter four, of course, was not comparable to any 1965 Mustang engine. The six, however, was exactly the same powerplant offered on the '65 (except the early cars that used the 170-cid unit). The 255 V-8 was derived from the 302, which, in turn, was developed from the 289, which itself was enlarged from the original Mustang's 260. Yet both the six and V-8 got better fuel mileage than their 1965 counterparts.

What the comparisons didn't show was the long, long road Mustang had traveled in 15 years. Along the way it had become one of the world's fastest four-place pro-duction cars—and too large, too unwieldy and too wasteful. That the lighter, more efficient 1980 Mustang so closely re-sembled the '65 in size and performance was perhaps a coincidence.

Then again, maybe it wasn't. We had had a lot of automotive decisions to make in the late Sixties and, looking back, it seems we too often made the wrong ones. Most enthusiasts agree that Mustang changed for the worse after 1970.

But hindsight is cheap and far too easily indulged. Enthusiasts could take heart from the 1980 Mustang. It proved that Americans could build a nimble, hand-some, efficient automobile that could be quite entertaining over the twisty bits. After 15 years, the original ponycar had come full circle.

During 1980, Ford gave every indication that it was about to get its performance act back together and put it on the road. And Mustang would definitely be the star of the show. Hinting at what might lie ahead was a tantalizing "concept car" that toured the show circuit that season: the Mustang IMSA. Powered by a much-modified version of the turbo-four, it sat astride massive Pirelli P7 tires nestled under

The 1981 Mustang added reclining backrests to the standard bucket seats and a T-top roof to the options list.

outlandishly flared fenders, matched by a deep front air dam, loop rear spoiler, and racy-looking pop-riveted plastic covers on side windows, back panel and headlamps. In name and appearance, it strongly suggested that Ford was more than just thinking about a return to competition—and about the International Motor Sports Association GT series in particular.

Then, in September 1980, Ford announced formation of a Special Vehicle Operations department (SVO). Significantly, it was headed by Michael Kranefuss,

newly arrived in Dearborn from his post as competition director for Ford Europe. SVO's stated purpose was to "develop a series of limited-production performance cars and develop their image through motorsport." It quickly got down to business with a turbo Mustang to be driven in selected 1981 IMSA GT events by former Porsche pilot Klaus Ludwig. Other Mustangs receiving similar direct factory help were a Trans-Am car for Dennis Mecham and an IMSA Kelly American Challenge racer for Lyn St. James.

As if to signal its return to the track, Ford debuted the McLaren Mustang in late 1980. The work of designers Todd Gerstenberger and Harry Wykes, this was a heavily modified Mustang with enough built-in potential for easy adaptation to race duty. Looking somewhat like the IMSA show car, the McLaren sported a grille-less nose above a low-riding "skirt" spoiler, functional hood scoops, tweaked suspension (mostly a mixture of heavy-duty off-the-shelf components), massive fender flares, and premium European BBS

alloy wheels wearing broad-shouldered 225/55R-15 Firestone HPR radial tires. Power was again provided by the turbo-four, but fitted with a new variable boost control. This provided a maximum boost range of 5 to 11 psi, as opposed to the stock engine's fixed 5-psi pressure. At 10 psi, rated output was 175 bhp at 2500 rpm, a considerable jump over the stock mill's, which was usually pegged at around 131 bhp (Ford never released official ratings for its turbo-four). A $25,000 price tag and virtual hand construction limited the number of copies to only 250 (including the prototype).

All this muscle-flexing came too late to affect the 1981 Mustang, which was little changed visually or mechanically. Reclining backrests were added to the standard bucket seats, interior trim was upgraded in appearance and completeness, and power door windows and a T-bar roof with twin lift-off glass panels lengthened the options list. The turbo engine was now limited to manual transmission only.

A five-speed overdrive manual gearbox had been announced as an option for both Mustang fours in mid-1980, and this became more widely available for '81. This pulled a shorter, 3.45:1 final drive (versus the four-speeder's 3.08:1 cog) for better off-the-line snap. The overdrive fifth was geared at 0.82:1 for economical highway cruising. It was just what the base Mustang needed.

Except for one thing: In adding the extra gear, Ford goofed. As we noted at the time: "Our biggest objections to the five-speed are its linkage—stiff, yet vague—and its shift pattern. As with the four-speed, first through fourth are arranged in the usual H-pattern. But fifth is awkwardly located at the bottom of the dogleg to the right of and opposite fourth, instead of up and to the right....Why Ford did it this way is a mystery, but it makes getting into or out of fifth real work. Our guess is that the engineers wanted to prevent inexperienced drivers from accidentally engaging over-drive and needlessly lugging the engine, as well as to prevent confusion with the often-used third. If so, they've succeeded admirably."

Ford apparently felt most drivers would want to downshift from fifth directly to third, bypassing fourth. At least that's what one transmission engineer told us. A more logical reason was that putting fifth over

and up would have entailed excessively long arm reach. The factory's "official" explanation was that the U-shaped shift motion would better emphasize the economy benefits of the overdrive fifth gear. Whatever the reason, it just didn't work.

But even this annoyance would soon be forgotten. Performance was about to make a surprising comeback in embattled Detroit, and Mustang would lead the charge.

1979-81 MUSTANG AT A GLANCE

Model Year Production

No.	Model	1979	1980	1981
02 (66B)	2-door coupe	143,382	117,015	69,994*
03 (61R)	3-door coupe	108,758	86,569	68,111
04 (66H)	Ghia 2-door coupe	48,788	20,288	11,991
05 (61H)	Ghia 3-door coupe	31,097	17,192	12,497
	TOTAL	332,025	241,064	162,593

*includes 4418 units with "S" (economy) option

Prices/Weights*
($/lbs)

No.	Models	1979	1980	1981
02 (66B)	2-door coupe	$4494/2530	$4884/2606	$5980/2601
03 (61R)	3-door coupe	$4828/2612	$5194/2614	$6216/2635
04 (66H)	Ghia 2-door coupe	$5064/2648	$5369/2665	$6424/2665
05 (61H)	Ghia 3-door coupe	$5216/2672	$5512/2692	$6538/2692

*Initial model year retail prices. All figures exclusive of options.

General Specifications

	1979	1980	1981
Wheelbase (in.)	100.4	100.4	100.4
Overall length (in.)	179.1	179.1	179.1
Overall width (in.)	69.1	69.1	69.1
Std. Trans.	4-spd. man.[1] 4-sp./OD man.[2] 3-sp. auto.[3]	4-spd. man.[1] 4-sp./OD man.[2] 3-sp. auto.[3]	4-spd. man.[1] 4-sp./OD man.[2] 3-sp. auto.[3]
Optional trans.	3-sp. auto.	3-sp. auto. 5-sp. man.[4]	3-sp. auto. 5-sp. man.[4]

1 4-cyl.; 2 6-cyl.; 3 V-8; 4 4-cyl. only

Engine Availability

Type	cid	bhp	1979	1980	1981
ohc I-4	140	88	Std.	Std.	Std.
ohc I-4 Turbo	140	131	Opt.	Opt.	Opt
ohv V-6	171	109	Opt.	—	—
ohv I-6	200	85	Opt.[1]	Opt.	Opt.
ohv V-8	255	117	—	Opt.	Opt.
ohv V-8	302	140	Opt.	—	—

1 Replaced V-6 option mid-model year

The McLaren Mustang (*opposite, top*) featured a grille-less nose, low-riding "skirt" spoiler, functional hood scoops, stiff suspension, widely flared fenders, and a 175-bhp version of the turbo-four. It sold for $25,000, and at that price only about 250 were built. Meanwhile, more four-cylinder production versions of the '81 (*bottom*) received the five-speed overdrive manual, an important selling tool when the national economy was down and inflation was up. A base coupe now stickered at $5980; Mustang output skidded to 162,593 units.

CHAPTER NINE

1982-86:
The
Boss
Returns

Mustang enthusiasts welcomed the sophisticated fifth generation as a happy turn of events for their car. Though timely and popular, the Mustang II was not a ponycar in the traditional sense, even if it did serve to keep the Mustang name alive through the dark and difficult Seventies.

By the dawn of the Eighties, however, Detroit had learned to live with government-mandated emission controls, safety equipment, even fuel-economy standards, and could literally afford to concentrate again on more interesting things—like really exciting styling and performance. The '79 Mustang reflected this in returning to the concept of the memorable '65 original, albeit reinterpreted for an even more challenging age.

By rights, ponycars shouldn't have survived to the Eighties in any form. And indeed, most didn't. The Plymouth Barracuda, Dodge Challenger, and AMC Javelin

were all gone by 1975, never to be seen again; Mustang's Mercury sibling, the Cougar, was puffed up into a "personal-luxury" intermediate. But against all odds, the 1970 Chevrolet Camaro and Pontiac Firebird managed to hold on through decade's end, and with surprisingly few changes. They even enjoyed a strong sales resurgence. The reason, of course, was that after the first energy crisis, they were about the only American cars (other than Chevy's Corvette) offering anything like Sixties-style performance. The fact that their hottest models, the Z-28 and Trans Am, were the hottest sellers after 1975 didn't go unnoticed in Dearborn.

Ford Motor Company needed to be on its toes, because its financial situation by 1980 had become almost as desperate—though not nearly as well publicized—as Chrysler Corporation's. Echoing the late Forties, the firm faced another historic change of leadership at a time when its

future was anything but certain. Chairman Henry Ford II had announced his intention to resign, which he did, leaving many to wonder whether his successors could turn things around.

Inspiration in the executive ranks was sorely needed. Though sales had been good in recent years, profits were dwindling due to the high cost of a massive product overhaul, begun with the '78 Fairmont/Zephyr, that was necessary to keep Ford competitive in the Eighties. When the bottom dropped out of the market in late '79, the shortfall mushroomed into a major cash crisis.

Stockholders needn't have worried, though, because 1980 ushered in two highly experienced go-getters at the top: Philip Caldwell as chairman and Donald Petersen as president. Petersen's arrival was especially good news. Not only was he an avid and knowledgeable "car guy" like the now-departed Lee Iacocca, he had definite

ideas about Ford's future, particularly in the areas of design and performance.

Petersen's enthusiasm would soon be reflected in a dramatic new generation of Ford Motor Company products. Meantime, he put his stylists and engineers to work on giving existing models some of the old "Total Performance" flair that had worked sales magic in the Sixties. As a direct descendant of those times, the fifth-generation Mustang was naturally one of the first Fords to benefit.

Ads in 1982 blared out, "The Boss is Back!" And it was, except that Ford called it the Mustang GT (*both pages*). What was back was the 5.0-liter (302-cid) V-8, now in H.O. form with 157 horses and 240 lbs/ft torque. With its free-flowing exhaust and four-speed stick, the GT could thunder from 0-60 mph in under eight seconds.

The result appeared for 1982 in the form of a reborn Mustang GT powered by the most potent Ford small-block in recent memory. Ads blared, "The Boss is Back!" And how. Packing a healthy 157 horse-power, its new H.O. (High-Output) 302 carried a special camshaft adapted from a marine version of the long-running V-8, plus a larger two-barrel carb, a bigger and smoother exhaust system, and low-restriction twin-inlet air cleaner. Teamed exclusively with four-speed overdrive manual transmission, it made for the fastest Mustang in years. Claimed 0-60-mph acceleration was below eight seconds, but most magazines found actual times closer to *seven*.

Looking much like the Cobra package it replaced, the GT came only as a hatchback with the top-grade TRX suspension, front and rear spoilers, foglamps, blackout treatment inside and out, console, luxury seat trim and other goodies, all for a

reasonable introductory price of $8308. The hot H.O. engine wasn't tied to the GT, being available for other models at $402 extra with the TRX suspension or $452 without. Still, GTs undoubtedly accounted for the bulk of installations. Incidentally, the tame 4.2-liter V-8, now in its final year, was available for the GT as a $57 credit option, though few buyers were likely penny-wise and performance-foolish this way.

The '83 Mustang sported a redesigned front and rear end (*top*). The 5.0 GT (*right*) was billed as "One hot piece of American steel that just might leave competition chasing its shadow," true to the extent that a four-barrel carb boosted horsepower to 175. Later in the year a Turbo GT (*above*) appeared. Its 2.3-liter four boasted multi-port fuel injection and 142 bhp.

H.O. apart, there was little to get excited about for '82. Model nomenclature was revised, with L, GL, and GLX hatchbacks and notchbacks arrayed below the GT in ascending order of price and luxury. A larger gas tank (up from 12.5 to 15.4 gallons), wider wheels and tires, and a remote-control lefthand door mirror were newly standard across the board. After compiling a poor reliability record, the turbo-four was withdrawn, though just temporarily, as it turned out. Other drivetrains stood pat save the optional

4.2-liter V-8, whose "mandatory option" automatic transmission got a fuel-saving lockup torque converter effective in all three forward gears, a device we'd see more of in coming years.

It's ironic that the best Mustang since the original arrived on the eve of what became one of the worst sales periods in Detroit history. But the market slump that began in 1979 bottomed out by '82, the year hot new GM competition arrived in a totally restyled, somewhat smaller third-generation Camaro/Firebird. Yet despite

all this, Mustang fared fairly well for a three-year-old design. Model year production totaled about 130,500 against some 179,000 of the all-new Camaros and 116,000 Firebirds.

With their 5.0-liter V-8s, tuned chassis, and race-inspired styling touches, the GT, Z-28, and Trans Am were quickly matched up in "buff book" comparison tests. While the GM cars won points for their superior handling and arguably more modern design, the Mustang was judged more practical for everyday use. And it was

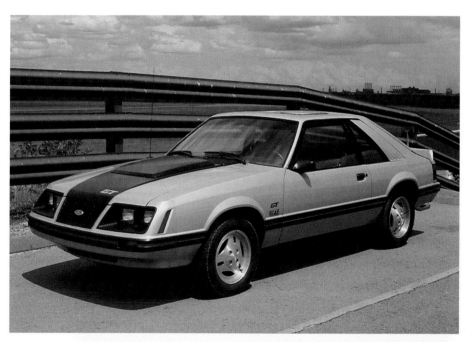

discernibly quicker. *Car and Driver* reported 0-60-mph times of 8.1 seconds for the GT against 8.6 seconds for the injected V-8 Camaro with automatic and a comparatively sluggish 10.6 seconds for the carbureted V-8 Trans Am with four-speed. Writing in the magazine's August 1982 issue, technical editor Don Sherman noted that "...in terms of sheer visceral appeal, [the Mustang] is right up there with the Porsche [928]"—high praise indeed.

Not all was sweetness and light, however. In testing the GT's sister ship, the RS version of the Mercury Capri (the domestic Mustang twin that replaced the European Capri for '79), CONSUMER GUIDE® magazine's staff found the power-assisted rack-and-pinion steering irritatingly vague, overly light, and lacking in feel. Wet-weather traction was a problem because of the V-8's ample torque: 240 pounds/feet, developed at a low 2400 rpm. We found it possible to light the back tires easily in brisk take-offs, accompanied at times by rear-end jitter that made us wonder what would happen in hard cornering on bumpy

The Mustang GT hatchback for '83 (*opposite, top*) listed at $9328. The 302-cid V-8 (*bottom*) was labeled H.O. for High-Output. After an absence of a decade, a convertible rejoined the Mustang lineup, available either as a GT or a more luxury-oriented GLX (*below*). The GLX was priced at $9449 and came with a 112-bhp 3.8-liter V-6 as standard. The GT ragtop retailed for $13,479 and came with the H.O. V-8. Convertible sales got off to a good start: 23,438 units for the model year, good for about one-fifth of total production.

surfaces. *CD*'s Sherman echoed our concerns: "In left-hand sweepers, the gas pedal acts as a power-oversteer switch....That smooth two-step unfortunately turns into a jitterbug in right-hand bends, where power hop conspires to make life difficult."

Despite such faults, Ford's latterday performance ponycar had much to recom-

mend it. We judged its interior not only more practical but roomier than Camaro/Firebird's. Though all three cars were hatchbacks, Ford somehow managed to provide a good deal more usable luggage space than GM. We also liked Dearborn's manual gearbox for its much lighter shift action (and more comfortably placed

shifter) compared with the truck-like Camaro/Firebird linkage. Our staff divided on driving position, some preferring the snug, low-slung stance of the GM cars to the more upright "vintage" openness of the Ford products. Yet most agreed the Mustang/Capri was a far better compromise for those who had to contend

with the daily drudgery of stop-and-go traffic, where the manual-shift Camaro/ Firebird was tiring to drive for any length of time. There was still work to do, but our overall view was that the revived 302 V-8 had given Ford's new-wave muscle car a much-needed dose of pizzazz.

Somebody in Dearborn apparently took road-test criticisms to heart, because a number of changes made the 1983 GT more competitive with Camaro/Firebird in the renewed ponycar performance wars. They began with wider-section tires, including newly optional 220/55-390 Michelin TRX covers, plus a slightly larger rear anti-roll bar, softer rear spring rates,

Ford pointed out that the new Mustang convertible featured rear-quarter windows and a zip-out glass rear window, features the '82 Chrysler and Dodge convertibles didn't have. Ford further mentioned that *all* of the windows could be lowered, a jab at the VW Cabrio, whose rear-quarter windows remained stationary at all times.

stiffer bushings for the front control arms, and revised shock valving. Higher-effort power steering was also included, for better high-speed control.

Speaking of speed, the H.O. V-8 was boosted to 175 bhp for '83 via a new four-barrel carb, aluminum intake manifold, high-flow air cleaner, enlarged exhaust passages, and minor valvetrain modifications. Even better, it mated with Borg-Warner's new T-5 close-ratio five-speed gearbox, the same one used in the Camaro/Firebird, which answered complaints about poor gear-spacing on the wide-ratio four-speed it replaced. All this plus a shorter final drive (3.27 versus 3.08:1) made for even faster takeoffs.

Mustang was also treated to a minor facelift for '83, its first since '79. The most obvious change was a newly rounded nose bearing a sloped, slightly vee'd horizontal-bar grille, good for a 2.5-percent reduction in aerodynamic drag. Running-horse emblems gave way to blue Ford ovals, taillights were restyled, and there were the usual trim and color shuffles.

Further emphasizing Mustang's return to performance, the extra-cost 4.2-liter V-8 was dropped and the 200-cid straight six was replaced as the step-up power option by the new lightweight "Essex" V-6 that had been introduced in other Ford models for '82. A 3.8-liter (232-cid) overhead-valve design, the Essex arrived at a rated

105 bhp with two-barrel carburetor (versus 88 bhp) and 181 lbs/ft torque (against 158). The 2.3-liter four, still standard for all but the GT, gained a more efficient one-barrel carburetor (replacing a two-barrel), plus long-reach spark plugs for fast-burn combustion, a move aimed at

Ford billed the Ghia-developed Mustang RSX (*above left*) a "one-of-a-kind rallye-sport two-seater." The 5.0 V-8 could be ordered on the '84 LX ragtop for $727 extra (*above*). In mid-1984 Ford trotted out a specially equipped Mustang GT-350 20th Anniversary model (*below and opposite*).

Ford's Special Vehicle Operations inspired the 1984 Mustang SVO, a sophisticated turbocharged *gran turismo* fastback with a decidedly European orientation.

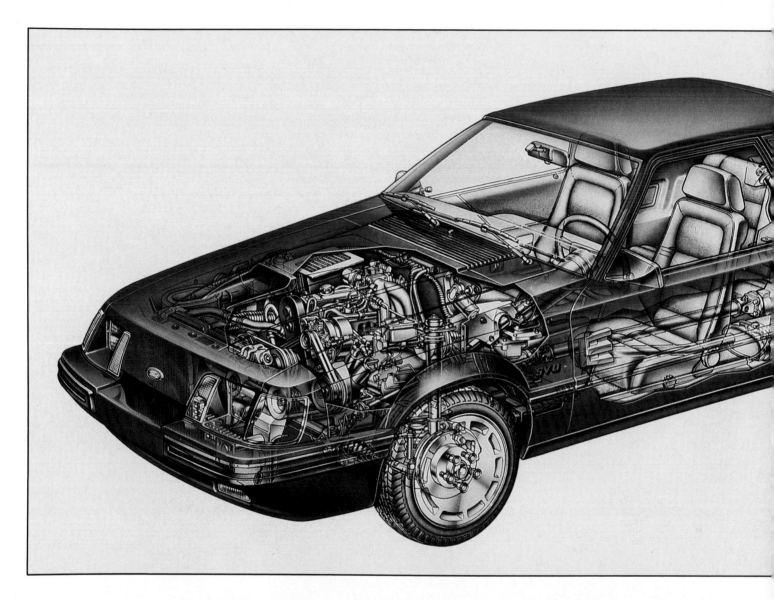

reducing emissions while improving warmup and part-throttle engine response. Curiously, these changes boosted alleged horsepower by five, to 93 bhp, though the rating would fall back to 88 the following year.

Newly standard for all '83 manual-shift Mustangs was a Volkswagen-like upshift indicator light. Reflecting the fuel jitters of 1979-80, this was an economy aid that signaled the driver when to shift to the next higher gear, based on the fact that an engine is usually most fuel-efficient when running at relatively low revs on wide throttle openings. It was a useful innovation, if hardly in the free-spirited Mustang tradition.

Other 1983 alterations included revised seat and door trim for all models, a

standard roller-blind cargo cover for hatchbacks, easier-to-read gauge markings, and less interior brightwork. A new sport seat option with mesh-insert headrests replaced the extra-cost Recaro buckets, which hadn't sold well. Reflecting its new concern with aerodynamics, Ford also deleted the hatchback's liftgate louvers and the notchback's Carriage Roof from the options list.

But the most glamorous '83 development by far was the first Mustang convertible in 10 years, available only in top-line GLX trim. Since the early Seventies, a number of small companies had been doing good aftermarket business by snipping the tops from Mustang notchbacks (and other cars) to satisfy a small but steady demand for top-down motoring.

Ford decided to get in on the action itself.

Like the Buick Riviera and Chrysler LeBaron ragtops announced at about the same time, the Mustang was an out-of-house conversion, a notchback coupe modified and trimmed (including top installation) by independent contractor Cars & Concepts of Brighton, Michigan. Like the Riv but unlike the LeBaron, the ragtop Mustang had roll-down rear side windows and a tempered-glass rear window. It was available with any drivetrain save the four-cylinder/automatic combination. As the first open-air ponycar in a decade, it added another dash of excitement to an already impressive Mustang lineup.

That lineup expanded at mid-season with a new Turbo GT hatchback and convertible, powered by the newly reengi-

neered version of the hyperaspirated 2.3-liter "Lima" four developed for this year's slick Thunderbird Turbo Coupe. The principal changes involved junking the carburetor for Bosch port electronic fuel injection and positioning the turbocharger upstream of the induction system so as to "blow through" it rather than "draw down" from it.

The cutaway drawing (*above*) shows some of the engineering features of the '84 SVO. It boasted unique styling features (*top right*) and a 2.3-liter intercooled turbo four that cranked out 175 horsepower (*right*). It ran the 0-60 mph sprint in 7.5 seconds and topped out at 134 mph.

Ford's latest electronic engine control system, EEC-IV, governed injector timing, idle speed, wastegate operation, supplementary fuel enrichment, engine idle, and emissions control. Other upgrades ran to forged-aluminum pistons, valves made of a special temperature-resistant alloy, lighter flywheel, die-cast aluminum rocker cover, and an engine-mounted oil cooler. Per usual turbo practice, compression was lowered from 9.0:1 to 8.0:1, and premium unleaded fuel was recommended for best performance. The result: 145 bhp at 4600 rpm—only 5 bhp up on the previous version but better than the magic "1 horsepower per cubic inch" ideal—and 180 lbs/ft torque peaking at a relatively low 3600 rpm.

Aside from slightly different nameplates, the Turbo GT was a visual twin to its V-8 running mate. Blackout trim, beefy Eagle GT performance radials, aluminum wheels, sport bucket seats, a businesslike gauge cluster, and five-speed manual gearbox were standard for both, and the GT suspension was tuned to match each engine. Packing the same horsepower Chevy advertised for its base Z-28, the Turbo GT could run 0-60 mph in well under 10 seconds and the standing quarter-Mustang for '85 sported a cleaner-looking front end, which was inspired by the SVO. The GT hatchback listed at $9885, the last year that customers would be able to buy a GT for under $10,000. Horsepower was up to 210.

mile in about 16 seconds while returning 25 mpg overall. But the T-Bird TC could match all those numbers, and the fortified 5.0-liter Mustang could now fly to 60 in near six seconds flat.

So though it seemed to offer the best of both worlds, this improved turbo Mustang proved no more popular than its 1979-81 predecessor. Aside from the fact that you couldn't get it with automatic or air conditioning—a severe drawback for many buyers—it cost $250 *more* than a comparably equipped V-8 GT. Yet it was slower, and with a peakier, less torquey engine, had to be driven that much harder. Ford said a late introduction and restricted availability limited Turbo GT sales, and only 483 of the '83s were built. But the real damper is best expressed by that time-worn Detroit adage, "There's no substitute for cubic inches"—not even high technology.

Nevertheless, Ford massaged its turbo-four even more, perhaps worrying that the latest energy crisis might get worse. (It wouldn't.) The result appeared for 1984 in yet another new performance Mustang called SVO. Engineered by Ford's Special Vehicle Operations section, hence the name,

this very special version of the Turbo GT hatchback boasted a lengthy list of modifications that read like a hop-up artist's wishbook. Notable were an air-to-air intercooler and the first-ever use of electronic control to vary boost pressure, which ranged up to 14 psi, then said to be the highest on any production turbo engine.

The '85 GT hatchback (*opposite, top and center*) weighed in at 2899 pounds, only 44 pounds less than the ragtop (*above*). The latter went out the door for $13,585. The electronically injected 302 V-8 (*opposite, bottom left*) turned out 180 bhp, 30 less than the carbureted version. Articulated sports seats were new to the GT.

These and other changes produced a claimed 20 percent more power—175 bhp at 4500 rpm, remarkable for a middling-size four—and 10 percent more torque—210 ft/lbs at 3000.

Also included among the SVO's mechanical exotica were a cockpit selector switch that "tuned" the engine's electronics to the grade of fuel being used, and special dampers to resist drivetrain rocking under full power. Putting that power to the ground was a five-speed manual gearbox with special Hurst linkage and a standard Traction-Lok limited-slip differential with 3.45:1 final drive.

SVO chassis revisions were equally thorough. In place of the stock 9.0-inch rear drum brakes were beefy 11.25-inch-diameter discs working in concert with front discs enlarged from 10.06 to 10.92 inches. New "aero-style" cast-aluminum wheels, massively sized at 16 x 7 inches, carried meaty V-rated European Goodyear NCT radials, later switched to P225/50VR-16 Goodyear Eagle GT50s with unidirectional "gatorback" tread (as on the '84 Corvette). Spring rates and bushings were stiffened, premium Koni adjustable shocks replaced the stock dampers, the front anti-roll bar was thickened (from 0.94 to 1.20 inches) and a rear bar was added, along with an extra inch of front wheel travel. The stock rack-and-pinion power steering was changed from variable-ratio to fast constant-ratio gearing, but retained high-effort valving for better road feel.

Setting SVO apart from lesser Mustangs were a distinctive "biplane" rear spoiler made of polycarbonate plastic, a unique grille-less nose (engine air entered from below the bumper and through a small slot above, making this a "bottom breather"), a large hood scoop to feed the intercooler, and dual square headlamps instead of the normal Mustang's smaller quads. A deep front air dam incorporated standard foglamps, and small "spats" or fairings at the leading edges of the rear wheel openings helped smooth airflow around the fat tires.

New for the Mustang GT for '85 were P225/60VR15 Goodyear Eagle unidirectional Gatorback tires on 15 × 7-inch cast aluminum wheels. The GT undercut the SVO by over $4500 and thus proved far more popular.

251

Inside, the SVO boasted such driver-oriented accoutrements as left footrest, brake and accelerator pedals spaced for easier heel-and-toe shifting, an 8000-rpm tachometer, turbo-boost gauge, and multi-adjustable seats like those in the T-Bird Turbo Coupe. Also included were electric rear-window defroster, tinted glass, AM/FM stereo radio with speaker/amplifier system, leather-rim tilt steering wheel, and the familiar Mustang console with graphic warning display. Only six major options were listed: air, power windows, cassette player, flip-up glass sunroof, and leather upholstery.

The SVO was perhaps the closest thing to a European-style GT yet seen from America, and the best-balanced high-

performance Mustang ever. Handling was near-neutral, cornering flat and undramatic, steering direct and properly assisted, braking swift and sure. Performance was exhilarating: 0-60 mph in about 7.5 seconds, the quarter-mile in just under 16 seconds at around 90 mph, top speed near 135 mph—real dragstrip stuff.

But in the end, it was just another sophisticated screamer that buff books liked and buyers didn't. At over $16,000 out the door, the SVO looked too expensive

In mid-1985 the SVO received flush aero headlamps, while internal tweaks to its turbo engine upped output to 205 bhp. None of it helped sales, however, which came in at 4508 for '84, 1954 for '85, and 3382 for 1986. After that, the SVO was dropped.

next to the V-8 GT, which delivered similar style and sizzle for a whopping $6000 less. Ford thus retailed fewer than 4000 for the model year, though annual build capacity was almost four times that.

Between them, the V-8 and SVO killed off the Turbo GT after fewer than 3000 hatchbacks and about 600 convertibles were run off for 1983-84. All early-'84 GTs, both V-8 and Turbo, were virtual '83 reruns save the new split rear seatback applied to most standard Mustang hatchbacks, and substitution of solid front head restraints for the previous open type. Several welcome running changes occurred starting in December 1983: revised accelerator/brake pedal spacing to facilitate heel-and-toe shifting, staggered rear shocks for reduced axle tramp in hard takeoffs, foglights integrated with the front spoiler, a restyled rear spoiler, and first-time availability of the turbo package for the convertible.

Trouble was, gasoline had not only become plentiful again but was selling at prices that were actually *dropping* in some places—many folks just couldn't resist the urge to splurge on a good old-fashioned V-8. This illustrated a peculiar irony of the Eighties: the renewed popularity of

relatively large-displacement engines at a time when automakers were discouraged from selling them by government regulations now out of synch with market forces and a worldwide oil glut. It was all too bad, for the Turbo GT was an honest attempt at reconciling performance with

economy, a worthy goal in any age and certain to remain one of the touchstones of our long-term automotive future.

Mustang's other changes for '84 were comparatively minor. A base-trim three-door joined the existing two-door model; GL and GLX equipment was combined

into a single LX trim level, available for all three body styles; and the fun-loving convertible was newly offered in GT as well as LX form, bringing total ragtops to three (including the aforementioned Turbo).

This year also brought a second 302 V-8, with throttle-body electronic fuel injection (TBI) and 10 fewer horses than the H.O. (165 total). It was reserved for non-GTs with automatic transmission, which now came in two forms as well: the familiar three-speeder and Ford's corporate four-speed unit, whose overdrive top gear allowed use of a shorter (numerically

Motor Trend saw the updated mid-1985 SVO as "a night-to-day improvement....We are mainly seduced by its high-revving, big hearted little motor and its precise tight-coupled controls. Its drivetrain has all the appeal of a Formula Atlantic car: intense, demanding, rewarding...and *fun*."

higher) final-drive ratio (3.27:1 versus 2.73:1) with no ill effects on mileage. TBI was also applied to the V-6 option, bringing it to 120 bhp and 205 lbs/ft torque; here, three-speed SelectShift was now your only transmission choice. In line with a widening industry trend, all manual-shift Mustangs received a starter interlock that prevented accidental lurching should you forget to depress the clutch pedal before starting.

Mustang reached the ripe old age of 20 in 1984—time really *does* fly when you're having fun—and Ford ran off 5000 copies of a special edition to mark the occasion. Reviving the famed GT-350 designation

from the Shelby days (see Chapter 11), it was officially a trim option for the convertible and hatchback, distinguished by "Shelby White" paint set off with maroon rocker-panel stripes but otherwise little different from the normal GT. It was a nice remembrance, but the legal department forgot to clear the name with Mr. Shelby, who claimed he owned "GT-350" and had been promised that Ford wouldn't use it without his okay. Carroll, by now working again with his old friend Lee Iacocca at Chrysler, may have been thinking of it for one of the hot Dodges he was building at his small-scale production

facility in California. In any case, he was miffed enough to hit Ford with a copyright infringement suit. Sometimes, it just doesn't pay to be sentimental.

Mustang sales seemed a pretty good barometer of the general market and the economy as a whole, bottoming out at just under 121,000 for 1983 before moving up again. The total was near 142,000 for '84, and would go above 156,000 for '85. By contrast, Camaro/Firebird sales, though initially much higher, began trending down, and by 1987 would be below those of Ford's veteran ponycar.

Which is quite remarkable when you

remember that the Mustang was an older, boxier design with a less sophisticated chassis and somewhat lower handling/roadholding limits. Yet these apparent minuses were actually pluses. Many buyers preferred the Mustang's more traditional on-road behavior, and earlier amortization of tooling costs allowed Ford to keep prices somewhat lower than GM could, even though the end of a decade-long inflationary spiral was helping both companies in that regard. But Ford also seemed to build its cars better each year—GM didn't—and kept improving them, too.

With all this, Mustang emerged as an uncommonly good performance value by mid-decade. For instance, 1985 prices ranged from just $6885 for the basic LX notchback to $13,585 for the top-line GT convertible and $14,521 for the slow-selling SVO. Though quite a bit above the '79 models in raw dollars, those figures were mighty competitive, especially once a strengthening yen began escalating prices on four-cylinder Japanese sporty compacts that couldn't match the V-8 Mustang for performance or charisma.

Both those qualities were further enhanced for '85. Low-friction roller tappets and a new high-performance camshaft lifted the carbureted H.O. V-8 to 210 bhp, an impressive 35-bhp increase. Similar changes brought the injected 302 (still

The '86 Mustang LX hatchback, here with the $1120 package that included the 5.0 V-8 and upgraded suspension, started at $7189. The hatchback continued to be the most popular of the three body styles, accounting for about 52 percent of 1986 production.

restricted to automatic) to 180 bhp. As before, the H.O. was available only with five-speed manual, which came in for revised internal ratios and a more precise, redesigned linkage. Rounding out GT improvements were beefier P225/60VR-15 "Gatorback" tires on seven-inch-wide cast-aluminum wheels, both borrowed from the SVO, plus gas-pressurized front shock absorbers and an extra pair of rear shocks (as a further aid to controlling axle tramp in hard acceleration).

Elsewhere, the cheap L versions were cancelled and remaining models acquired an SVO-style front-end cap with integral air dam and a simple air slot above the bumper. The SVO itself returned at mid-year with flush-mount headlights, newly allowed by the government (and pioneered by Ford among domestics with the '84 Continental Mark VII), plus an air-to-air

intercooler that added 30 bhp to the turbo-four, now rated at 205 bhp. The latter was also applied to a short-lived revival of the Turbo GT, which vanished again after minuscule sales. Its vastly more popular V-8 brother continued to trade points with Camaro/Firebird in magazine showdown tests. In all, Mustang attracted about 15,000 additional buyers for the model year.

Sales spurted to nearly 224,500 for 1986, a decade production high achieved with few changes. The main one was adoption of sequential port fuel injection for a single 302 V-8 rated at 200 bhp and available with either five-speed manual or four-speed automatic. The rear axles were strengthened to handle peak torque that now stood at a mighty 285 lbs/ft, and viscous (fluid-filled) engine mounts, introduced on SVO the previous year, were adopted for both V-8 and V-6 models.

Ford's continuing attention for practicality was evident in such improvements as a longer anti-corrosion warranty, increased use of sound-deadening material, and a more convenient single-key locking system.

The inevitable annual price increases were still evident, too, but, all things considered, were fairly modest. The notchback LX was up to $7295, the GT convertible to $14,220. The SVO was still around—and costlier at $15,272—but its days were numbered. With sales that had always been far below even Ford's modest projections, it was just too unprofitable to sustain, and would not return for '87. Model year production was 4508, 1954, and 3382 for 1984-86, respectively—9844 in all, barely half the available volume for a single year. The good news is that such rarity, coupled with unique specifications and high performance, makes for an

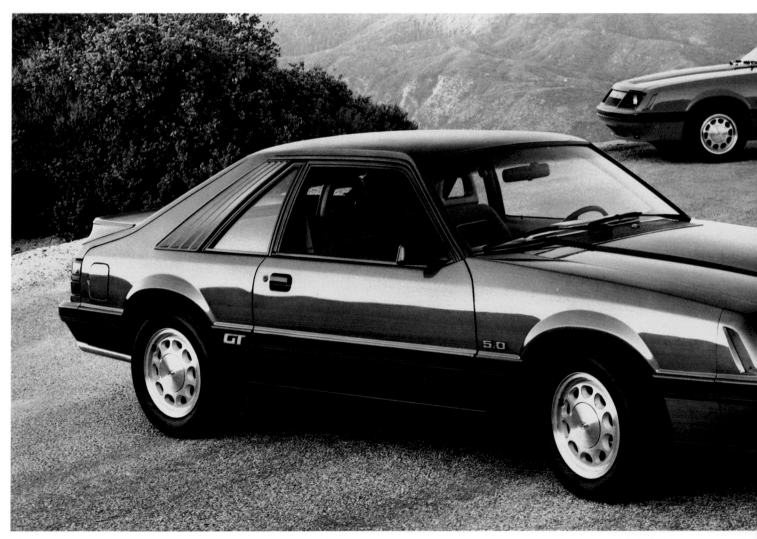

enthusiast's machine you can drive with pride into the distant future—and all the way to the bank.

But though it ranks among the least successful of modern Mustangs from the commercial standpoint, the SVO demonstrates the versatility and staying power of the winning fifth-generation design. And there was still more excitement to come as the original ponycar galloped toward its milestone 25th birthday in 1990. For that story, you need only turn to the next chapter.

"Mustang GT blends performance with fun," is the way Ford put it in 1986. The 5.0 V-8 now boasted multiple-port electronic fuel injection and 200 bhp.

1982-86 MUSTANG AT A GLANCE

Model Year Production

Model	1982	1983	1984	1985	1986
L/GL 2-door coupe	45,316	—	—	—	—
GLX 2-door coupe	5,828	—	—	—	—
GL 3-door coupe	45,901	—	—	—	—
GLX 3-door coupe	9,926	—	—	—	—
GT 3-door coupe	23,447	—	—	—	—
All 2-door coupe	—	33,201	37,680	56,781	106,720[1]
All 3-door coupe	—	64,234	86,200[2]	84,623[2]	117,690[2]
All convertible	—	23,438	17,600	15,110	
TOTAL	130,418	120,873	141,480	156,514	224,410

1 includes convertibles
2 includes SVO: 4508 (1984), 1954 (1985), 3382 (1986)

Prices/Weights ($/lbs)

	1982	1983	1984	1985	1986
L 2-door coupe	$6345/2568	$6727/2684	$7088/2736	—	—
GL 2-door coupe	$6844/2585	$7264/2743	—	—	—
LX 2-door coupe	—	—	$7290/2757	$6885/2657	$7189/2795
GLX 2-door coupe	$6980/2600	$7398/2760	—	—	—
L 3-door coupe	—	—	$7269/2782	—	—
GL 3-door coupe	$6979/2622	$7439/2788	—	—	—
LX 3-door coupe	—	—	$7496/2807	$7345/2729	$7744/2853
GLX 3-door coupe	$7101/2636	$7557/2801	—	—	—
GT 3-door coupe	$8308/2597	$9328/2969	$9578/3013	$9885/3063	$10691/3139
GT Turbo 3d coupe	—	$9714/2855	$9762/2869	—	—
LX convertible	—	—	$11849/3020	$11985/2907	$12821/3044
GLX convertible	—	$12467/2807	—	—	—
GT convertible	—	$13479/2975	$13051/3124	$13585/3165	$14523/3269
GT Turbo cvt	—	—	$13245/3004	—	—
SVO 3-door coupe	—	—	$15596/2992	$14521/2991	$15272/3140

General Specifications

	1982	1983	1984	1985	1986
Wheelbase (in.)	100.4	100.4	100.4	100.4	100.4
Overall length (in.)	179.1	179.1	179.1	179.3[1]	179.3[1]
Overall width (in.)	67.4	69.1	69.1	69.1	69.1
Standard trans.	4OD man	4OD man	4OD man	4OD man	4OD man
Optional trans.	5OD man 3 auto	5OD man 3 auto	5OD man 3 auto 4OD auto	5OD man 3 auto 4OD auto	5OD man 3 auto 4OD auto

1 SVO: 180.8 in.

Engine Availability

Type	cid	bhp	1982	1983	1984	1985	1986
ohc I-4	140	88	Std.	Std.	Std.		
ohc I-4 Turbo	140	145[1]	—	Opt.	Opt.[2]	Opt.[2]	—
ohc I-4 Turbo	140	205	—	—	—	—	2
ohv I-6/1 bbl	200	88	Opt.	—	—	—	—
ohv V-6/2 bbl	232	105	—	Opt.	—	—	—
ohv V-6 TBI	232	120	—	—	Opt.	Opt.	Opt.
ohv V-8/2 bbl	255	111	Opt.	—	—	—	—
ohv V-8/2 bbl	302	157	3	—	—	—	—
ohv V-8/4 bbl	302	175	—	3	3	—	—
ohv V-8 TBI	302	165	—	—	Opt.	—	—
ohv V-8/4 bbl	302	210	—	—	—	3	—
ohv V-8 TBI	302	180	—	—	—	Opt.	—
ohv V-8 PFI	302	200	—	—	—	—	Opt.[3]

1 rated 155 bhp 1985; 2 standard Turbo GT 1984-85, SVO; 3 standard GT

Note: TBI = throttle-body fuel injection; **PFI** = port ("multi-point") fuel injection; **bbl** = barrel(s) (carbureted engines)

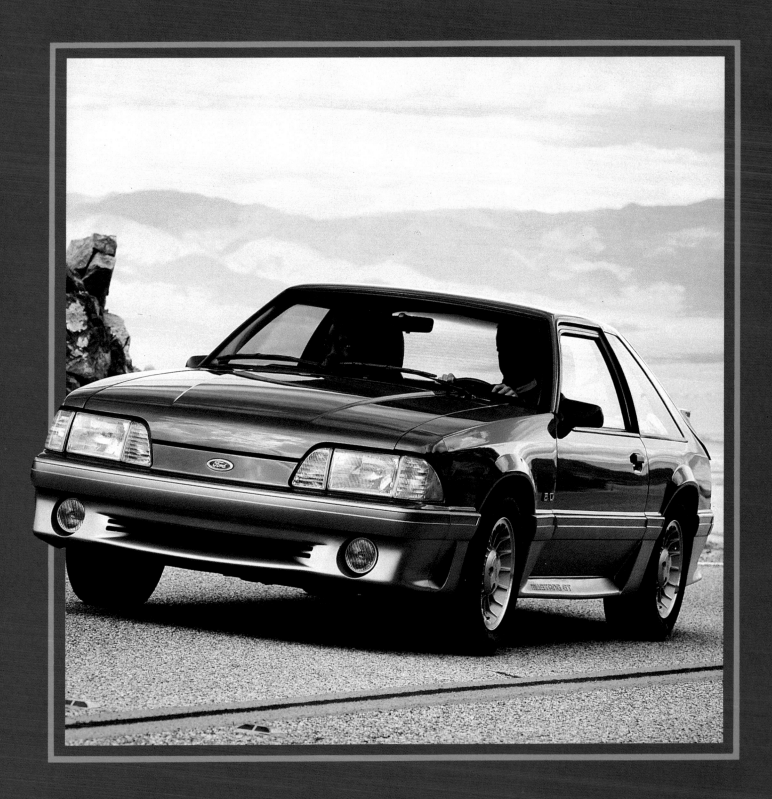

CHAPTER TEN

1987-89:
Galloping
into
the Future

Had Ford followed conventional Detroit wisdom, the fifth-generation Mustang would have been replaced by 1987, if not sooner. Though still popular heading into its eighth model year, and a vivid performer in GT guise, the basic '79 design was looking dated next to the newer Chevy Camaro/Pontiac Firebird—let alone some sporty Japanese coupes that were newer still.

But Ford had lately become a very *un*conventional car company, reaping many rewards from not following said "wisdom." From near disaster in the early Eighties, Ford roared back to record profit levels with a combination of bold product initiatives and demonstrably improved workmanship. By 1987, Ford was earning more money than even giant General Motors, despite building half as many vehicles. Critics were confounded, stockholders relieved, the automotive press impressed.

The fifth-generation Mustang played its part in this resurgence, but was clearly a car of Ford's past, not its future. Like Chrysler under Lee Iaccoca, Ford under Don Petersen had of necessity become more efficient, closing old factories, modernizing others with heavy investments in automated manufacturing equipment, slashing overhead in other areas, and laying off workers (only to rehire some of them later). But where Chrysler put all its chips on a single, if adaptable, basic platform, the compact K-body, Ford introduced new designs only where needed. Older models like Mustang would be kept on so long as their sales held up, which the company fostered with carefully considered improvements. What nobody could predict was how long the fifth generation might go on before a major overhaul or even a replacement was needed.

Meantime, Ford had set out to be the industry leader in aerodynamic styling, and for a very practical reason: Reducing air drag improves fuel economy. (Remember that CAFE was still a fact of life in the mid- and late Eighties, even if the standards weren't as rigidly enforced.) Not coincidentally, this commitment gave Dearborn designers a theme around which they could evolve a distinct and distinctive new corporate look. Ford execs had correctly reasoned that in an age of diminished automotive expectations, as the late Seventies and early Eighties surely were,

styling was more important to sales than ever. Sure enough, amidst a sea of mostly square-rigged Chrysler products and GM's growing "genericar" fleet, buyers flocked to smooth, unmistakable new Dearborn offerings like the 1983 Thunderbird and the Euro-style '86 Taurus—proof that standing apart from the herd sometimes puts you in front of it.

For all that, performance and not styling had been the key to Mustang's sales climb after 1982. Of course, that emphasis

wouldn't have worked without the advent of reduced inflation, lower interest rates, higher employment, rising personal income, and the steep drop in gas prices brought about by a worldwide oil glut, all of which contributed to a big upsurge in hot-car demand. At the same time, a whole new generation that hadn't been around for the original Mustang phenomenon was reaching car-buying age, and they craved sporty performance every bit as much as their "baby boomer" parents still did.

The heavily revised '87 Mustang took on the aero-look that Ford had debuted on the '83 T-Bird; it sported aero headlamps, new front and rear fascias, and a more modern instrument panel. The 225-bhp V-8 (with GT suspension) cost $1885 extra on the LX (*above*).

With another potentially vast buyer group at hand, plus rising sales in an economy newly returned to prosperity, the fifth-generation Mustang might well have been left alone—as indeed it pretty much was through 1986. Yet Ford knew as well as any Detroit producer that no car, no matter how popular, can last forever. The march of technology and the ever-changing market make that impossible. If the basic '79 package was still galloping along, it was only for the same reasons that gave the second-generation Camaro/Firebird their remarkable 12-year run: a sound basic design adroitly updated from time to time without losing the essential "American" character that still appealed to so many buyers—and that no foreign foe could match.

Trouble was, Mustang had become something of a "throwback" car selling at least partly on nostalgia, which was hardly in keeping with the high-tech image Ford sought to portray via aero styling and other advances. The company also started wondering what would happen to Mustang

sales should the market suddenly reverse itself again, not to mention the kind of sporty cars competitors were planning.

These and other considerations formed the backdrop for work toward a sixth-generation Mustang that began as early as 1982. Given the economic conditions of the day, the predictable consensus was that this ponycar for the Nineties would need to be smaller and lighter than the existing model—more like the old Mustang II or European Capri—with a shape obviously born in the wind tunnel, front-wheel drive for maximum space inside, and a new range of high-efficiency, overhead-cam four-cylinder engines to replace the low-tech ironmongery of the traditional V-8.

But just a year into this program, Ford decided to start over and collaborate with its new Japanese partner, Mazda. Ford had recently acquired a 25-percent stake in Mazda, whose small-car expertise was undeniable—at least equal, if not superior, to Ford's own. Mazda was then laying plans for the successor to its first front-drive 626 series, which included a sporty

coupe. Dearborn figured it might save money and end up with a better new Mustang by getting in on this project. The result would be two cars, each with its own styling identity and sold through separate dealerships but sharing basic chassis, running gear, and some inner structure. Making the idea even more attractive was Mazda's decision to build cars at a new plant in Flat Rock, Michigan (not far from Ford's historic River Rouge operations), and to make part of its output available to Ford.

It seemed a marriage made in heaven. Ford would get a new Mustang for a fraction of the cost of developing it alone; building it for Ford made Flat Rock more economically feasible for Mazda. And lest

Up front, the '87 Mustang GT (*both pages*) sported a lower air dam with integrated foglamps. "Mustang GT" was molded into the flared rocker panel moldings and the rear fascia covered the bumper. At the rear were "decorator" taillights and, for the hatchback, a large decklid spoiler.

we forget, Mazda, like other Japanese makers, really *needed* to build cars in America, not least because a worsening yen/dollar relationship was threatening to price its wares right out of the market. A U.S. production base would also foster a "good citizen" image, deemed necessary to help appease a Congress that had lately been threatening protectionist legislation amid hysterical reports of Japanese "dumping."

What Ford hadn't counted on was a storm of protest from Mustang loyalists once word of the joint venture leaked out. A new Mustang was a good thing to be sure, maybe even overdue. But *Japanese* engineering? Unthinkable! Sacrilege! No car was more all-American than Mustang.

The '87 Mustang GT (*below*) came with P225/60VR16 Goodyear Eagle GT Gatorback tires mounted on aluminum wheels. The LX (*right*) could be ordered with styled road wheels for an extra $178. The GT convertible listed at $15,724, the LX ragtop for $12,840.

How dare you put the name on a badge-engineered import! And looky here, Ford: Front drive may be okay for little econoboxes, but everyone knows that *real* performance cars—like BMWs and Ferraris—put power to the pavement with the *back* tires. Why, even the latest Camaro/Firebird have rear drive.

Though the decision came almost at the eleventh hour, Ford took heed and decided to release the once-and-future "Mazda Mustang" as the 1988 Probe (after its memorable Eighties series of aerodynamic show cars). It's not been on the market very long as we write this, but it's generated a lot of interest—especially its styling,

which makes Mazda's MX-6 version seem stodgy. In fact, Ford people assigned to the project at Mazda's Hiroshima headquarters reported that the Japanese kept referring to the Dearborn car as "the pretty one."

But having driven a couple of Probes, including both the 145-horsepower turbocharged GT model and the normally

aspirated 110-bhp LX, we can honestly say that it just wouldn't have been accepted as a Mustang. It's capable and spirited, but despite its all-Ford styling, the Probe is just too "foreign" to pass as a ponycar (an American invention, after all), new-wave or otherwise.

Fortunately for die-hard Mustangers, rising sales had already prompted Dearborn to rejuvenate its "real" ponycar, as it could well afford to once profits became embarrassingly large. The aim was not just to bring the old warrior in line with the corporate "aero look" but to keep it fully competitive in an increasingly competitive sporty-car market. If the end

Mustang for '88 saw only one change: a 540-amp battery for the LX (replacing a 460-amp unit). The LX two-door notchback (*below*) sold for $8726, making it the least expensive model in the lineup. The 90-bhp four was judged too weak for a 2800 pound car by CONSUMER GUIDE®, which recommended the $1885 5.0-liter V-8 package.

product also appealed to all those under-30s who'd missed the first act of the Mustang saga, so much the better.

Thus it was that the most fully overhauled Mustang in eight years arrived for 1987. The SVO was consigned to that great slow-sellers' parking lot in the sky (as was Mercury's Mustang, the Capri, which had been something of a sales disappointment since its '79 reincarnation), but other models returned: LX notchback and LX and GT hatchbacks and convertibles. The familiar fifth-generation shape was still clearly recognizable but slicker than ever, dominated by a smoother nose bearing flush-mount headlamps inboard of large wraparound parking/turn-indicator lamps. Rear side glass on closed models was pulled out to surrounding sheetmetal surfaces, taillamps were restyled, and most exterior brightwork was finished in black. Besides a more contemporary appearance, the sheetmetal reshaping made for more competitive drag coefficients: down to a claimed 0.40 for the notchback, 0.42 for convertibles, and 0.36 for the LX hatchback (the three-door GT tested out at a slightly blockier 0.38).

As before, GTs looked quite a bit different from LXs. The latter were more restrained, announced by a shallow "slot" grille between the headlamps, with a horizontal bar bearing a small Ford oval—a sort of smaller rendition of the Taurus's controversial "navel." Below this was a

body-color bumper with integral spoiler; wide, black rub strips flanking the license-plate mount were wrapped around to the front wheelarches, then carried back as lower-body protection moldings all the way to a color-keyed rear bumper. GTs seemed rather brash by comparison, with heavily sculptured rocker-panel skirts that looked like the adds-on they were, plus low-riding simulated scoops ahead of the rear wheels, a prominent faired-in spoiler on the hatchback, and multi-slotted "cheese grater" taillamps. At least the grille-less front was properly aggressive; it allowed air to enter via a wide "mouth" in a forward-jutting airdam that was flanked by round foglamps. So you shouldn't miss it, a big "Mustang GT" was molded into the rocker extensions and rear bumper cover.

Instrument panels are among the costliest components to change in a car, so the fact that all Mustangs had a new one for '87 was taken as a sign that the fifth generation might just hang around for more than another couple of years. The design could have come from Mazda, bearing a strong likeness to the latest 626

The little-changed '88 Mustang is seen here as a $9221 LX hatchback with the 5.0 V-8 option (*right*). The front-drive '89 Probe (*above*) was at first planned as a Mustang replacement, but strong demand kept Mustang alive.

dash. The right side was cut away at the top to form a useful package shelf (and a sense of greater interior spaciousness). On the left was an upright pod with a pair of rocker switches built in on each side for lights, hazard flasher, and rear-window defroster; wipers and indicators were left to steering-column stalks, and the cruise control buttons were still conveniently placed in the steering-wheel spokes. The wheel itself was also more modern, if slightly dull. Dropping down from dash center was a broad console housing large rotary controls for temperature, fan speed, and air distribution. A quartet of large, square vents marched across the dash rail. Modernization was also evident in new-design armrests, door panels, and seat adjusters.

The year's most noteworthy mechanical alterations involved the venerable small-block V-8 — no surprise, as it was now way ahead of the 2.3-liter four in customer preference. Induction changes, including a return to freer-breathing, pre-1986 cylinder heads, added 25 horses for a total of 225, thus matching output of the top Camaro/Firebird option, the 5.7-liter Corvette engine. Torque was up, too: to a mighty 300 pounds/feet. The 302 remained standard for GTs, which also received larger-diameter front disc brakes (10.9-inches versus 10.1) and a recalibrated front suspension.

As for the four, it finally shed the old one-barrel carburetor for multi-point electronic fuel injection, but was hardly any more potent at 90 bhp and 130 lbs/ft. However, it now teamed with standard five-speed manual or optional four-speed automatic overdrive transmissions (versus the previous four-speed stick and three-speed slushbox), which helped maximize what performance it could muster.

The big surprise was that the 3.8-liter V-6 option was no longer available, leaving a huge power/performance gap between the four and V-8. The obvious conclusion, as we pointed out in *Auto 1987*, was that "Ford clearly plans on selling mostly V-8-powered Mustangs this year."

The Mustang LX with the V-8 (*right*) got its own designation for '89: LX 5.0L Sport. It was basically a GT *without* the boy-racer spoilers and air dams. The LX ragtop stickered at $17,001, $511 less than the GT.

And so it did—only a lot of those V-8s were sold in LXs, as an $1885 package that included the GT's chassis and rolling stock. In fact, demand for 5.0-liter LXs proved so strong that Ford actually ran short of engines, telling buyers that if they wanted a V-8 Mustang, it'd have to be a GT. There were reasons for this rather odd situation. For some buyers, the facelifted GT was either ugly, outlandish, or both, which must have dismayed Jack Telnack (who took over from Don Kopka as Ford design chief in mid-1987). Others simply preferred their V-8 go in the quieter-looking LX because it was less likely to be noticed by the law.

Regardless, the newly fortified small-block provided blistering performance reminiscent of the so-called "good old days:" 0-60 mph now took slightly less than six seconds. This illustrates that technology was now allowing Ford (and others) to accomplish what it had once achieved only by adding cubic inches. For example, to get about 225 net horsepower in, say, a 1972 Mustang, you had to order an optional 351 V-8, which came in three versions spanning 168 to 275 net bhp. Yet the '87 small-block was more fuel-efficient and smoother-running from cold, demanded less maintenance, and was likely more reliable to boot. That, friends, is progress.

Of course, the price of progress is often high, but Mustang remained an exception.

"Though far from perfect—or perfected—the Mustang GT is put together well enough and offers a ton of go for your dough," we said in 1987. "Despite a full option load—air, premium sound system, cruise control and power windows, door locks and mirrors—our test car came to $14,352, which is an exceptional value when IROC-Z Camaros, Toyota Supras, and Nissan 300ZXs can go for $5000 more." To paraphrase an old adage, the more some things change, the more others stay the same.

Change in and of itself, however, does not guarantee success. Despite the extensive updates, Mustang saw substantially lower volume for 1987—over 65,000 units lower. Still, 159,000 sales was quite respectable, all things considered (the previous year's production spurt stemmed in part from rush buying in advance of revised tax laws that took effect with the start of calendar '87); the facelift, though costly, would be

CONSUMER GUIDE® magazine said that "for performance-minded buyers on a budget, nothing else delivers so much bang for so few bucks" as the '89 Mustang GT. The hatchback listed at $13,272.

amortized over the next few years.

Mustang has seen only token changes since '87. The sole alteration for '88 was a higher-capacity standard battery for LXs. For '89, Ford belatedly recognized customer styling preferences by making the LX V-8 package option a distinct model trio called LX 5.0 Sport, and threw in the GT's multi-adjustable sports seats. The only other change of consequence was standardization of the optional power windows and Power Lock Group for the two convertibles.

But wait: 1989 technically marks the 25th anniversary of Mustang's introduction. What about a commemorative special? Though one has been rumored through most of '88, Ford tells us that *if* it appears, it won't be until 1990. Why? Because by Ford's calendar, that's the right year. The company has always regarded the first Mustang as a '65 model and not (as some enthusiasts would have it) a "1964 ½."

What this silver anniversary Mustang might be like is somewhat hazier. Detroit's rumor-mongers first spoke of a GT with extra-heavy-duty suspension to handle a 351 V-8 (still in production for Ford trucks) with twin turbochargers and an alleged 400 bhp, a package engineered by factory-contract race-car builder Jack Roush. This,

however, has apparently been nixed because of high costs relative to the limited production planned, said to be as low as 2000 units.

A better bet seems to be a modified 302 GT with an extra 35-50 bhp via tuned intake runners and tweaked engine electronics, plus the usual suspension upgrades,

The '89 Mustang LX convertible (*above*) stickered at $14,140. New for the '89 LX ragtop were the GT's articulated sports seats. Standard equipment: five-speed manual gearbox, power steering and brakes, tinted glass, remote mirrors, console with armrest, AM/FM stereo, and complete instrumentation, including tach.

some different bolt-on body pieces for styling distinction and, some speculate, four-wheel disc brakes left over from the SVO. More exotic possibilities have also been reported, including the supercharged 3.8-liter V-6 from the '89 Thunderbird Super Coupe and a new double-overhead-cam 32-valve V-8. At this writing, Ford says it has no plans for a 25th-birthday special, but that seems about as plausible as dropping the Mustang. Whatever its final form, you can bet the limited edition will be another instantly collectible Mustang.

Which brings us to the end of the Mustang saga—so far. For whatever happens with that quarter-century commemorative, you can bet that Mustang will continue to be part of Ford's future. After all, it's been too much a part of Ford's recent past—too much a legend—to ever disappear, just like that other legendary Ford of modern times, the Thunderbird.

Of course, Mustang will continue to evolve, perhaps into something quite different from what we know today. Equally certain is that we *will* see a sixth generation—a genuine red-blooded all-American design this time—and perhaps not all that far down the road (though your guess is as good as ours as to precisely when). Meanwhile, we can look forward to further improvements in the versatile fifth-generation Mustang, whose excitement and sheer staying power have been among the more pleasant automotive surprises of the Reagan era.

Back in 1982, these editors concluded the Mustang story to that point with the following sentiments, which are no less true in 1989: "Nearly a generation after the first Mustang rolled out the door, it is pleasant to reflect that the same kind of car is with us today, with the same name and—despite safety, emission, and fuel economy regulations—much the same character. Following the tried-and-true pattern, there's still an options list long enough for you to tailor your Mustang as a mild-mannered runabout, thrilling European-style tourer, or anything in between. Other traditions—long-hood/short-deck shape, room in back only for occasional riders, and handsome bucket-seat interior—are also preserved. In fact, Mustang never looked better. The current models are clearly more sophisticated and more efficient than the 1965 original, yet

have the same spirited youthfulness that long ago infected a generation of car lovers with 'Mustang fever.' Today, there's a new generation looking for the same kind of excitement. And as has been the case for [over] 20 years now, they'll find it in the cars with the Running Horse."

To that, we can only add, may it always be so. Happy 25th birthday, Mustang. And many, many more.

1987-89 MUSTANG AT A GLANCE

Model Year Production

	1987*	1988[1]	1989[1]
All 2-door coupe	64,704	—	—
All 3-door coupe	94,441[2]	—	—
All convertible	—	—	—
TOTAL	159,145		

1 not available at time of publication
2 includes convertibles

*Note: The above figures, like all in this book, are from Ford production records, but other sources paint a slightly different picture. *Ward's Automotive Reports*, for example, published the following for 1987:

All 2-door coupe	58,100
All 3-door coupe	80,717
All convertible	20,238
TOTAL	159,055

Prices/Weights
($/lbs)

	1987	1988	1989
LX 2-door coupe	$8043/2862	$8726/2894	$9050/2724
LX 3-door coupe	$8474/2920	$9221/2961	$9556/2782
LX convertible	$12840/3059	$13702/3081	$14140/3081
LX 5.0 Sport 2d	—	—	$11410/2894
LX 5.0 Sport 3d	—	—	$12265/2961
LX 5.0 Sport cvt	—	—	$17001/3214
GT 3-door coupe	$11835/3080	$12745/3193	$13272/3193
GT convertible	$15724/3214	$16610/3341	$17512/3341

General Specifications

	1987	1988	1989
Wheelbase (in.)	100.5	100.5	100.5
Overall length (in.)	179.6	179.6	179.6
Overall width (in.)	69.1	69.1	69.1
Standard trans.	5OD man	5OD man	5OD man
Optional trans.	4OD auto	4OD auto	4OD auto

Engine Availability

Type	cid	bhp	1987	1988	1989
ohc I-4	140	90	Std.[1]	Std.[1]	Std.[1]
ohv V-8	302	225	2	2	2

1 LX only
2 standard GT; optional LX (1987-88), std. LX "5.0L" series (1989)

The '89 Mustangs seen opposite are LXs. CONSUMER GUIDE® in *Auto '89* commented that the LX's four "is too weak," and recommended the LX 5.0L for those who preferred the LX's less gaudy styling. "A V-8 convertible is loads of fun and, like the Mustang GT, will no doubt be a collectible car years from now....mileage is nothing to crow about, but a V-8 Mustang is still the best of a vanishing breed." The LX could be a bit of a sleeper on the street.

CHAPTER ELEVEN

The Shelby-Mustangs 1965-70: Short-Lived Thoroughbreds

No Mustang history would be complete without a chronicle of the Shelby-Mustang, the inspired creation of one-time race driver Carroll Shelby. The first of this special breed, the GT-350, appeared barely a year after the production Mustang itself, and was quickly recognized as one of that elite group: the dual-purpose production car—brilliant on the street, superbly capable on the track. The impetus for it was Ford's desire to give the Mustang a solid performance image. And what better way to do that than by taking the Sports Car Club of America's B-production championship away from Corvette?

To some, the name Carroll Shelby still evokes memories of a disarming country boy with a wide "aw shucks" grin under a black cowboy hat. More knowledgeable enthusiasts remember him as the man who built the Cobra 289 and 427, the fastest street sports cars of all time. Shelby's rags-to-riches, back-to-rags, back-to-riches story is the stuff legends are made of.

At various times a truck driver, roustabout, ranch hand, salesman, and chicken farmer, Shelby began racing sports cars comparatively late in life. Beginning with MGs in the mid-Fifties, he soon progressed to Ferraris, Maseratis, and Aston Martins. He was a good driver, maybe even sensational. Still, sports-car racing was a gentleman's sport in those days. There was no prize money worth talking about, and drivers like Shelby who weren't independently wealthy had to have sponsors who'd supply a car and pay the expenses of racing it. Shelby, however, had no problem promoting himself or his driving ability, and he delivered on those promises time and time again. By the time he won the prestigious 24 Hours of Le Mans in 1959, he was on top of the world. Sadly, heart trouble forced him to retire as a driver in 1960.

Undaunted, Shelby settled in Southern California and made cars his business. First he bought a Goodyear tire distributorship, then started America's first high-performance driving school. All the while, he nurtured a private dream: He would build a car of his own someday—the world's fastest production sports car. But without capital and no firm design ideas, his vision remained only that.

Then fate took a hand. Shelby had heard that Ford was developing a small, lightweight V-8, the Fairlane 221 (later enlarged

to 260 cubic inches and eventually to 289). At about the same time, it appeared that A.C. Cars Ltd. of Surrey, England, would go out of business when it unexpectedly lost its supplier of engines for its strong, lightweight open sports car, the Ace. Shelby stepped in at precisely the right moment, dropped the Ford small-block into the A.C. sports car, and the Cobra was born.

Cobra and Shelby soon became household words—at least in car-enthusiast

households—and were inextricably linked with Ford's "Total Performance" program of the early and mid-Sixties. The reason: Cobras were winning almost every race in sight, including the coveted World Manufacturer's Championship for GT cars, a title that Ferrari had held for 12 years before grudgingly yielding it to Shelby.

With all this—and "Powered by Ford" badges—the Cobra became a performance legend with enormous potential image value

to Ford's regular product line. Dearborn had already discovered the youth market and had launched Mustang to capture it. But though initial sales had been higher than anyone at Ford expected, Mustang was still generally seen as a low-cost sporty compact and not a high-performance thoroughbred despite availability of the potent HP 289 V-8.

Accordingly, Ford asked Shelby to develop a Mustang-based racer capable of

besting the Corvettes in Sports Car Club of America (SCCA) competition. Flushed with the Cobra's success and knowing his way around racetracks and the sanctioning bodies, Shelby had a predictable reply: "Build a hundred of 'em." That was the minimum volume for a car to qualify (be homologated) for production-class events.

As a first step, Shelby built two proto-types from a pair of ordinary Mustang 2+2s. Led by race driver Ken Miles, who'd

Carroll Shelby, father of the Cobra roadster, and Ford got together to turn out a high-performance Mustang, the Shelby GT-350. Its mission was to bolster Ford's image with young buyers and to compete with the Corvette in road racing. It did, taking SCCA national road race championships in its class in 1965-66-67. Styling (*above a '66*) differed from the stock car and the 289 High Performance V-8 (*opposite*) was tweaked to 306 bhp. Note the Cobra valve covers.

helped develop the Cobra, and engineer Chuck Cantwell, a team of engineers and development drivers made numerous changes to transform the soft, boulevard cars into muscular racers that were still recognizable as Mustangs—important if Ford was going to reap any "race-proved"

publicity benefit from the exercise. Ford also saw the program as producing a Corvette-beater for the street. (Enthusiasts generally regarded the Cobra as an A.C. or a Shelby, not a Ford, even though it was sold through selected Ford dealers.)

With final specifications determined by

fall 1964, a dozen cars were built by hand at Carroll's small Cobra facility in Venice, California; all were completed by Christmas. Meantime, Ford's San Jose, California, assembly plant had shipped another 100 white fastbacks for conversion as regular assembly-line models, 88 of which were

finished by New Year's. Thus, when the SCCA inspectors arrived, they were somewhat surprised to find that more than the required 100 had been completed. The car's public unveiling came at Riverside Raceway on January 27, 1965.

For no particular reason, except maybe that it sounded good, Shelby designated his much-modified Mustang the GT-350, though it was also referred to as the Shelby-Mustang or simply Shelby GT. Two versions planned from the start: an S-model for the street and a full-house R-model for competition. However, it's important to

Shelby received partially finished Mustangs in his California plant. The '66s, in various colors, sported an altered grille with a Mustang emblem on the left, a fiberglass hood with functional air scoop, side scoops, and side stripes. The stripes over the hood, roof, and rear deck cost extra.

note that the GT-350 was conceived mainly for racing. The street car was simply a less extreme, more tractable derivative of it, and would naturally account for the vast majority of production. Shelby realized that he wouldn't be able to sell many *bona fide* racers, one reason the S ended up looking so much like the R. The other was Ford's desire for easy "product identification" between the racers and everyday Mustangs.

The GT-350 was a straightforward proposition and never a secret. It began with a white Mustang fastback built at San Jose with all-black interior, the 271-bhp "Hi-Performance" V-8, and Borg-Warner T-10 four-speed all-synchromesh manual transmission with Ford linkage and close-ratio gearing. Hood, exhaust system, and rear seat were all deleted. A beefier rear axle, borrowed from Ford's big Galaxie, was supplied in place of the stock Falcon unit to cope with planned increases in power and torque. This also brought larger, 10 × 3-inch drum brakes, which were fitted with metallic linings.

Shelby's small but professional workforce did the rest. Chassis changes began up front, with relocated suspension mounting points, a larger anti-roll bar, and the factory's optional front-disc brakes, made by Kelsey-Hayes. Also fitted was a heavy tubular steel brace between the tops of the front shock towers to eliminate body flex under high cornering loads. Trailing radius rods were added at the rear to provide more secure axle location, and Koni shocks were fitted all around. Rolling stock comprised hefty 15 × 6-inch Shelby-made wheels shod with 7.75 × 15 Goodyear Blue Dot performance tires. Steel-rim wheels with aluminum centers, supplied by Cragar to Shelby specifications, were optionally available. Finally, the low-geared stock steering box was replaced by a fast-ratio unit. All this gave the GT-350 near-neutral handling instead of the stock 2+2's strong understeer.

Underhood modifications comprised aluminum high-rise manifolds, finned aluminum valve covers and oil pan, wilder camshaft profile, and a larger Holley carb fed by a functional air scoop in a hood made of fiberglass instead of steel. These changes and a less restrictive exhaust system boosted the hi-po 289 to an honest 306 bhp. A Detroit "Locker" differential was specified to get power to the ground.

Interiors were decked out in true racer style: three-inch-wide competition seatbelts, tachometer and oil pressure gauge mounted at eye level on a stock Mustang dash, and a flat, wood-rim racing-type steering wheel. For better weight distribution, the spare tire was relocated to the vacant rear-seat area, mounted on a fiberglass shelf. Because of SCCA rules concerning passenger capacity in production-class racers, omitting the back seat enabled the GT-350 to run as a sports car rather than as a "sedan." For those who occasionally needed "+2" seating, Shelby offered a kit with a small rear bench that put the spare back in the trunk.

All 1965 GT-350s were painted white; no other colors were available. All Ford and Mustang insignias were removed, but blue rocker-panel stripes prominently displayed the GT-350 name. (America's international racing colors are blue and white.) Most early Shelbys also got the matching, extra-cost 10-inch-wide twin "Le Mans" stripes that ran from hood to rear deck over the top.

Not surprisingly, the R-model's most important distinction was a hotter engine, basically the racing Cobra unit. SCCA rules decreed that production-class cars could have suspension or engine modifications but not both. Shelby chose to

homologate the street suspension, leaving him free to use a more potent engine—a smart move.

Advertised as dyno-tuned and race-ready, the GT-350 competition mill was fully balanced and blueprinted. Ports were enlarged, polished, and matched to the combustion chambers; pistons were fly-cut; and a special camshaft was installed. Additional racing hardware was a high-volume oil pump, oil cooler, special tube headers that fed straight pipes, and special valve-cover breathers. Replacing the street model's carburetor was a 715-cfm Holley that gulped air though a spun-aluminum plenum chamber mated to the hood scoop. Horsepower was formidable: an estimated 340-360 gross. Completing the drivetrain was a Borg-Warner T-10 "Sebring" gearbox, offered with either aluminum or cast-iron case, mated to a steel-plate competition clutch.

Every GT-350R was track-tested at California's Willow Springs Raceway prior

The '66 Shelby GT-350 (*opposite*) stickered at $4600; 2378 were built. Note the hood locks and rear side windows. The first 252 GT-350s for 1966 (*above*) were actually leftover '65s updated to 1966 specs.

to shipment. The suspension was basically a heavy-duty version of the street setup, with competition rubber on American Racing Equipment 7×15 five-spoke magnesium wheels. A long-range 34-gallon gas tank with quick-release cap and large splash tunnel was used, and some cars received four-wheel disc brakes. Race-ready curb weight was only 2500 pounds, versus 2800 for the S-model.

Further weight savings came from an interior that was stark even for a track machine. Sound insulation, carpeting, door panels, window winders, dash padding, ashtray, and glove compartment were all left out, of course. The only glass was in the windshield; light-weight Plexiglas substituted in door windows (with aluminum frames) and the backlight. A rollbar and safety harness were fitted per racing practice, and almost everything was finished in matte black. The driver sat in a fiberglass racing bucket padded in black vinyl. Controls were limited to switches for ignition, lights, and wipers, plus a bank of "CS" competition gauges. The last, from left to right, showed fuel pressure, oil temperature, speed (0-160 mph), revs (0-8000 rpm), oil pressure, and water temperature.

Outside, the stock front bumper and gravel pan were scrapped for a one-piece fiberglass apron that provided a rudimentary airdam. A large central slot ducted air to the oil cooler; two smaller flanking holes likewise served the front brakes. Early

GT-350Rs retained the stock rear bumper, painted white to match the body, but this was later left off entirely.

The GT-350R was homologated for SCCA B-Production, which meant it would compete against small-block Corvettes, Sunbeam Tigers, Jaguar E-Types, and the occasional Ferrari or Aston Martin. Out of 562 completed as 1965 models, no more than 30 were built to racing specifications. However, all the special parts were available over the counter, per Shelby

The '66 GT-350H saw a production run of 936 units. Hertz Rent-A-Car ordered them mainly for the publicity value. Most were black with gold stripes and differed from other GT-350s by virtue of Magnum 500 14×6 steel wheels. Hertz didn't approve, but some of these rental cars went racing on weekends!

philosophy, so anyone could turn a street car into the racing version by simply removing and/or substituting components —as indeed some did.

Arriving at $4547, about $1000 more than a standard V-8 Mustang and an equal amount less than a Corvette, the S-model GT-350 was in the middle of the performance market but ahead on the road. With 0-60 mph times averaging 6.5 seconds, a top speed of 130-135 mph, and racecar handling and braking, it drew rave reviews. At $5950, the R-model was even more of a bargain: ready to race—and win—right off the showroom floor.

And win it did. On Valentine's Day 1965, Shelby American served notice that the only time a Corvette would see Victory Circle was when there were no GT-350s around. Sure enough, the Mustang with a Cobra's bite notched three class wins in its very first outing. It didn't entirely dominate B-Production in 1965 (a Corvette 327 eked out the Southwest region championship), but the bulk of the '65 season and all of 1966-67 was a Shelby-Mustang parade. To wit:

B-Production National Champions 1965-67

1965 Central: Robert Johnson, GT-350

Midwest: Brad Brooker, Kansas, Corvette/GT-350

Northeast: Mark Donohue, New Jersey, GT-350

Pacific: Jerry Titus, California, GT-350

Southwest: Zoltan Petrany, Texas, Corvette

1966 Walter Hane, Florida, GT-350

1967 Fred Van Buren, Mexico City, GT-350

Such frequent success made it logical to assume that a lot of GT-350s were competing, but it was actually the same relative handful of cars winning time after time. And since the racers looked so much like the street cars, many assumed they were all alike under the skin, too. They weren't, of course, which was a real ego boost for S-model owners.

Shelby had arranged to sell Cobras through a network of performance-oriented Ford dealers, and they now eagerly took on the GT-350. Though billed as "not the car for everybody," it left showrooms as rapidly as it left stoplights. Demand quickly exceeded the production capacity of the Shelby plant, which was

also still building Cobras, prompting the newly named Shelby American Inc. to move from Venice to two huge hangars at Los Angeles International Airport by the spring of 1965.

Virtually every major publication reported on the GT-350 once the first batch of street cars was made available for press testing. As the Shelby had no obvious competitors, most journalists could do little more than describe the car and its sizzling performance. Most found it loud, rough-riding, and a real effort to drive, but they loved its instant response. Function was the key word. Anything that didn't fit the prime purpose—to go fast, handle well,

Note the license plate frame on the Shelby GT-350H above: "Rent-A-Racer." Hertz claimed that it lost money on these high-performance rental cars, but apparently the publicity value was quite a plus because Hertz continued to rent Shelby Mustangs in 1967 and '68, although these cars didn't wear special GT-350H badging.

and stop quickly—had been either modified or thrown out.

Glowing press reports and stellar track performances made the GT-350 as much an overnight legend as the Mustang that sired it, and other automakers were quick to copy, putting scoops and rocker-panel stripes on all sorts of ordinary production models. But none of these cosmetic imitators was in the same league.

One of the Shelby-Mustang's lesser-known racing efforts came in the National Hot Rod Association. During May 1965, some members of the GT-350 project team began exploring the idea of a car designed for NHRA's B/Sports Production class. Carroll's earlier "Dragonsnake" dragster had put the Cobra in the public eye. It seemed logical that a properly set up GT-350 could do the same for Mustang.

Evaluation and development were turned out to famed race-car builder Bill Stroppe, and NHRA promptly approved the engine modifications deemed necessary: machine-ported heads with big valves (1.88-inch intake, 1.63-inch exhaust), heavy-duty valve springs, drag headers, and complete balancing and blueprinting. It was soon decided, however, that "customer" cars would carry the stock 306-bhp powerplant, with the full-tilt mill available only over-the-counter—and to all factory entrants, of course. This arrangement not only enabled Shelby to keep price down but also avoided hard feelings should a customer blow up the expensive factory engine. NHRA also approved a trunk-mounted scattershield, mandatory for a car with solid lifters. A clutch and pressure plate designed for dragstrip duty were also certified, which meant that they could be installed at the factory, saving owners the time and expense of doing so later.

Other modifications evolved as the project progressed. Cure-Ride 90/10 uplock shock absorbers appeared up front, Gabriel 50/50 downlock shocks at the rear. Stroppe also designed a set of ladder-bar torque arms and specified a Hurst "Competition Plus" shifter. He checked every loophole in the NHRA and AHRA (American Hot Rod Association) regulations, but some of his proposed modifications just wouldn't fit the rules. These included lengthened front spindles, modified seat tracks, re-radiused rear wheels, and repositioned front upper control arms. Stroppe even considered a

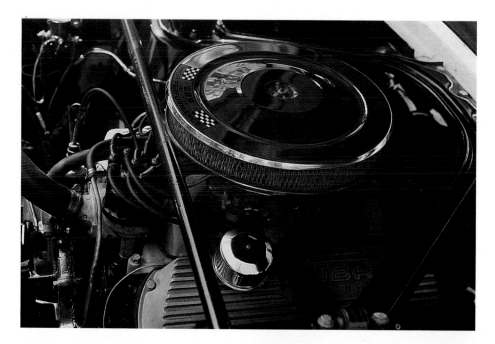

Weber-carbureted, roller-cam Factory Experimental engine, but it never went beyond bench testing.

The first GT-350 drag car was built and sold to a Shelby dealer in Lorain, Ohio, in August 1965. A second was bought and run by Mel Burns Ford of Long Beach, California. Though the total number built is not known, most were officially '65s, though a few 1966 models were similarly converted.

Meantime, decisions in Dearborn were affecting plans for the 1966 Shelby-Mustang. The exotic mid-engine Ford GT, developed to carry the company's colors in the world's most prestigious endurance events, was faltering, so the effort was turned over to Carroll Shelby. Since the company had invested a lot of money and faith in Shelby American, it expected a tangible return: an all-conquering Ford GT. Shelby thus had a lot more on his mind for 1966 than just his fortified Mustangs.

The '65 Shelby was an exciting, hairy-chested performer, but as a two-seater it was impractical for the enthusiast with a family. The noisy, lurching, Detroit Locker rear end howled and clunked at low speeds, which unnerved many people; the side-exit exhaust was not only loud but illegal in some states; and the policy of "any color you want, so long as it's white" was an obvious sales limitation. From Ford came a demand for something called cost-effectiveness (justifying the cost of each

item or modification by potential sales). Meantime, the Shelby people tried to explain roadability to accountants.

As a result, the 1966 GT-350 was more a product of customer surveys and Ford planners than Carroll Shelby. In concept and as a finished car, it wasn't the sort of thing he'd have built had the choice been his alone. Buyers seemed to want performance all right, but they didn't want to give up other automotive virtues. Thus did the Shelby GT begin evolving away from Carroll's original concept and toward something with broader market appeal—a car more like the standard Mustang and less like the race-going original.

Because Shelby didn't always incor-

porate specific changes with the first car of a new model year, using up parts on hand before ordering new ones, there is no clear distinction between the 1965 and 1966 GT-350s—appropriate for a limited-production manufacturer. The first 250 or so '66s were thus leftover '65s with all the new-model cosmetic changes, including revised grille, side scoops, and Plexiglas rear quarter windows.

When actual '66 production began, color choices expanded to include red, blue, green, and black, all set off with white racing stripes. At the same time, the Mustang fastback's extra-cost fold-down rear seat became a Shelby option as well. Almost all the '66s had it, and for an

obvious reason: It was easier and more profitable for Ford to leave it in than for Shelby to replace it with that fiberglass shelf. The same rationale prompted the battery to be left in its stock underhood position.

Heavy-duty Ford-installed shock absorbers were retained, as were the special Pitman and idler arms that gave the '65 its sharp steering. All '65 and early '66 cars had rear traction bars running from inside the chassis rails to the top of the rear axle; later '66s were fitted with Traction Master underride bars. Early cars also had lowered front A-arms, which altered the steering geometry for improved cornering, but this was deemed to be uneconomical and was

eliminated on later '66s.

Engines and drivelines stayed mostly the same, too. The Detroit Locker rear end was made an option—as was automatic transmission. Like most '65s, all '66 Shelbys had front disc brakes and large rear drums with sintered metallic linings.

The 1965 and '66 Shelby GT-350s (here a '66) are considered the "purest" of the Shelby Mustangs. They put the emphasis on performance and handling at the expense of ride and comfort. They were difficult to drive, but they were as close to a race car as one could buy off the showroom floor.

These were high-effort binders, but they just didn't fade, even though cooling area diminished somewhat with a switch to 14-inch wheels, either chrome styled steel or cast-aluminum alloy at the buyer's option. All '66s received Plexiglas rear quarter windows in place of the stock fastback's louvers, which improved over-the-shoulder vision.

If the '66 Shelby wasn't as loud or fierce as the '65, Carroll kept things interesting with a Paxton centrifugal supercharger as another new option. (A special blown model was envisioned but never actually released.) Sold factory-installed at $670 or as a $430 kit, the blower was said to boost horsepower by "up to 46 percent"—to beyond 400 bhp—which allegedly cut the 0-60-mph time to a mere five seconds. Few cars were so equipped, however.

Increased production was planned for 1966 so every dealer who wanted cars could get them. Shelby also sold the Hertz company on the idea of renting out 1000 specially trimmed GT-350H models, finished in black with gold stripes. Hertz did so at major airports throughout 1966, but a good many were returned after weekends with definite signs of competition fatigue. Not surprisingly, Hertz found the program a mite unprofitable, and called it off after this one year.

Total 1966 Shelby-Mustang production was 2380, including 936 Hertz models and six specially built convertibles that Shelby gave to friends as gifts. No racing cars were constructed, though a few '65 leftovers were registered as '66s. Shelbys continued to race and win that season, but were essentially the same cars that had run the year before.

Overshadowed by the GT-350's stunning success in SCCA "club" racing during this period was its performance in the Trans-American Sedan Championship. First run in 1966 and essentially an offshoot of SCCA's sedan-class events, The Trans-Am was intended as a series of "mini-enduros" ranging anywhere from 200 to 2400 miles and two to 24 hours, thus requiring pit stops for fuel and tires. As planned, it attracted Mustangs, Barracudas, Falcons, Dodge Darts, and a host of under-2.0-liter imports. By the end of its inaugural season, the Trans-Am had become one of the most popular series on the SCCA schedule, due partly to a good many professional factory entries. To make things

more interesting, a manufacturer's trophy was awarded to the company whose cars won the most races. Driver egos took a back seat as each factory vied to establish or uphold its performance reputation.

Trans-Am rules were based on FIA Appendix J specifications for Series Production Cars (Group 1) or Touring Cars (Group 2). The senior class was limited to displacement between 2000 and 5000 cc (120-305 cubic inches), a maximum wheelbase of 116 inches, and minimal mechanical modifications. Only four-seaters were allowed, so the GT-350, officially a two-seater, wasn't. Mustang hardtops did the honors instead.

The 1966 schedule had seven races, but the series was very close all season and the winner wasn't decided until the finale at Riverside, California. There, a huge, blue Shelby-American race van appeared with a Shelby-ized Mustang hardtop for former GT-350 team driver Jerry Titus, editor of *Sports Car Graphic*. Titus qualified on the pole and won the race, thus giving Ford the manufacturer's trophy. But Shelby-American's eleventh-hour appearance signaled a change in Ford's racing priorities, probably due to the realization that the 1967 GT-350 would not be as competitive as the original R-model. From here on, the factory's Trans-Am effort would be carried out with Mustang hardtops.

Earlier that season, Shelby-American had extended race assistance to Mustang entrants—logical, as the notchbacks and GT-350s shared virtually all mechanical components. When this support was withdrawn (because somebody felt that there wasn't enough product similarity), Ford took up the slack with limited support of its own to outstanding non-Shelby teams. By season's end, therefore, Ford and Shelby-American were competing with each other.

The production Mustang became larger, heavier, and more "styled" for 1967, which meant the GT-350 would be too. To keep weight down and appearance distinctive, Ford's Chuck McHose and Shelby-American's Pete Brock created a special fiberglass front end to complement Dearborn's longer hood, with a yawning

The '66 Shelby GT-350 (*left*) received a conventional exhaust system that ended under the rear bumper instead of ahead of the rear wheels, as in 1965. Also, the springs were softened.

"mouth" grille bearing twin center-mount driving lamps (since moved outboard on some cars to comply with state headlight-spacing regulations). Functional, scoops were everywhere—hood, lower bodysides (for rear-brake cooling), and sail panels (for interior air extraction). Out back, a special trunklid with integral spoiler appeared above wide taillamp clusters purloined from the new Mercury Cougar. These touches plus Mustang's new full-fastback styling made the '67 Shelby a handsome, fast-looking car—more like a competition car than many racers. There was still nothing else like it.

Because the '67 Mustang was heavier than its predecessors, and with customers wanting a more manageable Shelby, power steering and power brakes were now mandatory options. Mustang's newly reworked interior was little altered for the Shelbys, though they received several unique touches: a distinctive racing steering wheel, additional gauges, and a genuine rollbar with built-in inertia-reel shoulder harnesses.

But this was only the half of it. With the big-block 390 V-8 the new top performance option for the '67 Mustang, Carroll, in typical fashion, decided to go Ford one better by substituting the physically identical 428 to create a second Shelby, the GT-500. It proved highly popular, out-selling its smaller-capacity stablemate two-to-one. The GT-350 still carried the 289 small-block warmed to Shelby specs. Horsepower was ostensibly the same as before but surely less in actuality, as the steel-tube exhaust headers and straight-through mufflers were eliminated.

Needless to say, less power and the weight of all that new fluff took a big toll on GT-350 performance. The GT-500 was predictably quicker, yet somehow disappointing. Carmakers began using more conservative horsepower ratings in 1967 as a sop to insurance companies. The Shelby's 428 was thus advertised at 335 bhp but probably had more. *Car and Driver*, whose test car took 6.5 seconds 0-60 mph, said that while the 428 "isn't the Le Mans winner," the GT-500 "does with ease what the old [GT-350] took brute force to accomplish." But *Road & Track*, which recorded 7.2 seconds in the same test, said the car "simply doesn't have anything sensational to offer....A [standard] Mustang with the 390 cu. in. engine option does as well." As ever, Shelby had an answer: an optional 427—which *was* the Le Mans engine—rated at 390 bhp, though few were ordered.

If the Shelby was still a wilder pony than Mustang, performance was now clearly taking a back seat to styling and luxury, mainly because that's where the money was spent. Ford was still spending it, of course, but was now more intimately involved with the Shelbys—and more determined that they turn a profit. And indeed, production was increased for '67, to 3225 units. But Shelby-American made no attempt to race any of them. Unlike the 1965-66 models, they just weren't cut out for the track.

Still, Ford didn't want to let its '66 Trans-Am championship seem like a fluke, so it backed a full-fledged Mustang victory team put together by Shelby-American for the '67 season. This consisted of two

Mustang received its first major restyling for 1967, and so too did the Shelby. It differed considerably from the stock model by virtue of a stretched nose that used a lot of fiberglass parts (including the hood), large side scoops, rear ducktail spoiler, and '67 Cougar taillight lens. The GT-350 (*right*) was rated at 290 bhp.

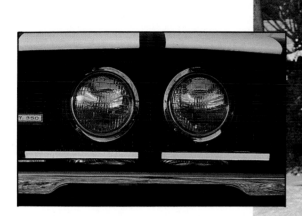

The '67 Shelby Mustang (*right*) boasted an integral rollbar and inertia-reel shoulder harnesses, the first in the U.S. auto industry. Also seen was a 140-mph speedometer and 8000-rpm tach.

canary-yellow hardtops with flat-black hoods running under the banner of "Terlingua Racing Team," an honorary team comprising the "sponsors" of Shelby's Terlingua (Texas) Boys' Ranch. Trouble was, Carroll had to contend with a rash of other new factory-backed teams. Stock-car ace Bud Moore fielded a brace of Cougars, Roger Penske a Camaro for former GT-350 pilot Mark Donohue, and well-known hotshots Dan Gurney, Parnelli Jones, George Follmer, Peter Revson, David Pearson, Ronnie Bucknum, and Jerry Titus had joined the fray.

In a season extended to 13 races, the Shelby-prepped Mustangs crossed the finish line often enough to give Ford the manufacturer's trophy for a second year. But the factory lavished most of its attentions on the Bud Moore Cougars, which got more financial consideration than other Ford teams, plus "trick" parts and drivers Gurney and Jones.

This may help explain why Carroll himself began tiring of the car business by 1968. His GT-350 had dominated SCCA competition, and his Ford GT effort had produced victories at Le Mans in 1966-67. But he'd seen several close friends lose their lives on the racetrack—and seen the sport become increasingly competitive and expensive. Meantime, the rapid march of technology was making it impossible for all but a few specialists to grasp new principles quickly and apply them successfully. Racing, Carroll decided, wasn't fun anymore, it was business. And building his own cars had lost much of its original

allure because Ford was now calling most of the shots.

Indeed, Dearborn's control over the Shelby-Mustang became total with the '68s. Production was moved from Los Angeles to Michigan, where stock Mustangs (supplied from Ford's Metuchen, New Jersey, plant) were converted into

Shelbys by the A.O. Smith Company under contract. Ford also took over all Shelby promotion and advertising.

Those ads provided more evidence of the steady shift from performance to plush. A modest facelift brought a full-width hood scoop and hood louvers, a larger grille cavity with square running lamps (not

driving lights), sequential rear turn signals and miscellaneous trim changes, plus new convertible alternatives with built-in roll-over hoop. Luxury options like air conditioning, tilt steering wheel, tinted glass, and AM/FM stereo now outnumbered performance features.

With federal emissions limits in force,

the GT-350 was switched to Ford's newly enlarged 302-cid small-block—and lost a lot of power, withering to a rated 250 bhp. The Paxton supercharger option returned from '66 to add about 100 horses, but again found few takers. The big-block Shelbys were still clearly preferred, out-selling the GT-350s by two-to-one.

The GT-500 initially retained its 428, re-rated to 360 bhp. A few, however, got ordinary 390 V-8s, reflecting a shortage of 428s due to an engine-plant strike. Buyers weren't told about the substitution, which was nearly impossible to spot. Mid-model year brought some redress in the GT-500KR (for "King of the Road"). This had

the new Cobra Jet engine, basically the 428 with big-port 427 heads, larger intake manifold and exhaust system, and an estimated 40 extra horses. Ford also tossed in wider rear brakes.

Shelby's 1968 volume was up for the fourth straight year—to 4450 units—but would go no higher. The press mostly yawned at what was becoming a cushy cruiser, and Ford made no effort to race the '68s. Not that they'd have been competitive. They'd grown too big, too soft, too heavy—not at all the race-bred stormers their predecessors had been. And Ford only managed to dilute their appeal further with Shelbyesque showroom Mustangs like the '68 GT/CS ("California Special") notchback. So though the Shelby-Mustang wasn't exactly finished by the end of '68, it didn't have long to live.

Shelby-American still had its eye on the Trans-Am in 1968. Group 2 rules had

become difficult to manage, so SCCA now bent them a bit. Engines were still restricted to 5.0 liters (305 cid), but minimum weight was set at 2800 pounds and wheels up to eight inches wide were allowed. The schedule again included 13 events. Though the Cougars were gone, Shelby's Mustangs and Penske's Camaros had to battle a pair of factory-backed AMC Javelins. The Shelbys were painted blue or red, had flat-black hoods, and ran under the "Shelby Racing Co." banner.

Titus, still the lead Shelby driver, finished first in the Daytona 24-hour opener. But Penske/Donohue started to click with round two, winning that race and the next seven before Titus broke the string at Watkins Glen. By that time there was no catching Camaro, which took the championship.

Other winds of change were definitely blowing, too. Emissions and safety regula-

tions were a new fact of life, as were insurance premiums reaching upwards of $1000 for 25-year-old males who drove hot cars. And changing buyer tastes caused performance to become less important than luxury.

Ol' Shel saw the handwriting on the wall. Ever the individualist, he'd begun by building the sort of car he himself wanted to drive. He didn't like decisions made by committees, where accountants and lawyers usually overruled engineers and test drivers. And the niche he'd created for his cars in the Ford lineup was now being filled by production models like the Mach 1 and Boss 302, both new for '69.

The '68 Shelby Mustangs received new front-end styling that inspired the design of the '69 Mustang; 1965 Thunderbird sequential taillights rode up back. The GT-350 (*both pages*) was powered by a 302-cid V-8, a stroked version of the 289 used from 1965-67. *Pages 302-303:* This 1968 GT-350 convertible was one of 404 built.

Mustang got a new bodyshell and heavily revised styling that year, and its Shelby relatives did, too. Fastback and convertible returned in GT-350 and 500 form, differentiated from the weightier, lengthier, much busier production car by a three-inch longer hood, reshaped front fenders, and a new nose with a big loop bumper/grille (all made of fiberglass to hold down weight). The Shelby also had a clipped tail still bearing a lip spoiler and Cougar sequential turn signals. Scoops were everywhere—five NACA ducts on the hood alone—and wide reflective tape stripes ran midway along the flanks. Said

Car and Driver's Brock Yates: "I personally can't think of an automobile that makes a statement about performance...any better than [this Shelby]."

The standard 302 V-8 (*opposite*) in the '68 Shelby GT-350 cranked out 250 horsepower. It used an aluminum intake manifold, Holly 600 cfm carb, and "Cobra" valve covers and air cleaner. A Shelby Cobra emblem adorned the steering wheel, while auxiliary gauges were mounted on the console (*below*). The hood scoops and vents (*right*) were for real.

GT. 500

Shelby had begun offering big-block 428 V-8s in the '67 GT-500. The '68 GT-500 V-8 (*above*) boasted 360 bhp, down from 400 in 1967 because the pricey dual-quad intake manifold and carbs were exchanged for a single Holley four-barrel on an aluminum intake manifold. The $4439 GT-500 fastback (*opposite*) saw a production run of 1140 units.

But brag is one thing, fact another. And the fact was that greater weight and stiffening emission controls rendered the '69s a lot tamer than any previous Shelby. The GT-500 was no longer a "King of the Road," but retained that '68 model's 428 Cobra Jet engine, still at a nominal 335 bhp, though actual output was down 25 horses by most estimates. The GT-350 was promoted to Ford's new 351 "Windsor" small-block, with hydraulic-lifter cam, big four-barrel carb, aluminum high-rise manifold, and low-restriction exhaust system. Advertised horsepower was unchanged from that of the previous 302—but then, this engine was standard in the new Mach 1 fastback, which cost much less than the Shelby.

Yates derisively described the '69 GT-350 as "a garter snake in Cobra skin." But if the magic was gone—and it was—part of the problem was that Carroll Shelby had long ceased to be involved with his cars. The

'69s, in fact, were built at Ford's Southfield, Michigan, plant right alongside box-stock Mustangs. With design now being determined by production economics and marketing studies, proposed features like fuel injection, moonroof, and reclining seats didn't stand a chance.

The other part of the problem was new competition from the Mustang line itself. The Mach 1 was interference enough, but mid-year brought the hot Boss 302, a thinly disguised Trans-Am racer for the street, and the incredible Boss 429, a thinly disguised drag racer stuffed full of Ford's potent "semi-hemi" big-block.

Of course, the Bosses were no cheaper or more readily available than the Shelbys. But they were "a curious duplication of effort," as Yates put it, and only dimmed what luster the Shelbys still had. "The heritage of the GT-350 is performance," Yates mused, "and it is difficult to understand why the Ford marketing experts failed

The '68 Shelby GT-500KR (*left*) replaced the GT-500 at mid-year. KR, of course, stood for "King of the Road." The difference was that a more powerful 428CJ V-8 replaced the 428. It was rated at 335 horsepower, but it actually pumped out about 400 horses. The fastback was priced at $4473 and 933 were built.

to exploit its reputation." But fail they did, and production sank by fully 25 percent, to 3150 units.

Back at the Trans-Am, rules changed yet again for the 12-race 1969 season, diverging even more from those for Group 2 sedans. Mustang fastbacks were now

legal, so the hot ticket was the new Boss 302, and Shelby's outfit prepared one apiece for Peter Revson and Horst Kwech. A second team fielded by Bud Moore had Parnelli Jones and George Follmer in the driver's seats. Massive factory engineering efforts now produced semi-tube frame

chassis (disguised as roll cages), acid-dipped bodies, huge tires, flared fenders, spoilers, wings, and mind-boggling horsepower.

The canted-valve H.O. engine made an impressive debut in the '69 curtain-raiser, where Jones was declared the winner after a post-race check of lap charts. Round

two, at Lime Rock, Connecticut, went to Sam Posey in a Shelby-prepared Boss 302. But it would be the Shelby team's only victory that year, and at Riverside on October 4, Carroll Shelby announced his retirement as racing-car developer and team manager.

At the same time, Shelby said goodbye to the car business, and not without reason. He was no longer involved in the design or production of the cars bearing his name, and other hot ponycars had caught up with the softer, slower 1968-69 Shelbys. Worst of all, his cars weren't even being

Opposite page: At $4238, the '68 Shelby GT-350 ragtop (*top*) cost $201 less than the GT-500 convertible (*bottom*). *This page*: The '69 Mustang received a new bodyshell, as did the Shelbys. The 428 V-8 carried over for the GT-500. The ragtop (*top*) sold for $4753, the fastback (*bottom*), $4434.

The '69 Shelby GT-500 (*right*) looked completely different from the front than regular production Mustangs, although the '71 Mustang would borrow the '69 Shelby look. The nose stretched out four inches longer than in '68, and since the front fenders differed from the Mustang, they were made of fiberglass. So was the hood, which sported three NACA-style air scoops up front and two air vents at the rear. Two air scoops graced each side of the Shelby and the rear spoiler was even more pronounced. The rear end again used '65 T-Bird taillights.

raced much any more.

Ford Division general manager Lee Iacocca also saw the end of the road, and agreed to end the Shelby-Mustang program. Cars still in the pipeline at the end of 1969 production were given Boss 302 front spoilers, black hoods, and new serial numbers to become "1970" models, a little over 600 in all. With that, the Shelby-Mustang was dead.

How ironic, then, that Trans-Am excitement peaked with the 1970 season. The Shelby team was absent, but at least half a dozen other big-league entries more than filled the void: Penske Javelins, Bud Moore Boss 302s, Jim Hall Chaparral Camaros, Jerry Titus Firebirds, Dan Gurney Barracudas, Sam Posey Dodge Challengers, Owens/Corning Camaros. Mustang ended up champion once again, beating all its impressive rivals.

But then the factories began backing away, possibly because there was simply too much competition now. This seemed to leave things wide open for many capable independents, but they quickly learned that the price of playing this game was astronomical. And with Detroit ponycars having become so much bigger and heavier, foreign makes like Porsche, Alfa Romeo, and Datsun started to win regularly. In a desperate attempt to bring back the large crowds of 1970, SCCA opened up the '71 Trans-Am to A-Production, B-Production, and A-Sedan: Corvettes, Camaros, Datsun Zs—even Cobras and GT-350s—all together. But it wasn't the same. The electricity of earlier seasons had all but disappeared.

Detroit was forced to redefine performance in the Seventies, and each succeeding year brought a less inspiring crop of cars with progressively less power and

longer 0-60 mph times. Yet it was precisely because of this that Carroll Shelby's very special Mustangs came to be appreciated all the more. Astute collectors began snapping them up as fast as they could, and values started to climb. Though there's still a good deal of confusion over what Shelby-Mustangs are worth, there's no disputing

their caliber. All are exciting, high-performance *gran turismos* of uniquely American character, born of a uniquely American passion for pavement-ripping power and blinding acceleration. Yet they also possessed world-class handling and, in later years, levels of luxury and reliability most foreign GTs were hard pressed to

match.

Carroll Shelby showed how much depth existed in Ford's basic ponycar package, and he did it with a style all his own. The Shelby GTs were first and foremost one man's idea of what Mustang could and ought to be. Today, as a generation ago, they remain the ultimate ponycars.

1965-70 SHELBY-MUSTANG AT A GLANCE

Model Year Production

Year	GT-350 fastback	GT-350 convertible	GT-500 fastback	GT-500 convertible	Total
1965	562	—	—	—	562
1966	2,380[1]	18[2]	—	—	2,398
1967	1,175	—	2,050	—	3,225
1968	1,253	404	2,073[3]	720[4]	4,450[4]
1969	1,085	194	1,536	335	3,150
1970	350		286		636

1 includes 936 GRT-350H models
2 includes 6 prototypes and 12 cars converted 1981 from restored convertibles
3 includes 933 GT-500KR models
4 includes 318 GT-500KR models

Prices/Weights
($/lbs)

Year	GT-350 fastback	GT-350 convertible	GT-500 fastback	GT-500 convertible
1965	$4547/2800	—	—	—
1966	$4428/2800	—	—	—
1967	$3995/2800	—	$4195/3000	—
1968	$4117/3000	$4238/3100	$4317/3100[1]	$4438/3200[1]
1969	$4434/3000	$4753/3100	$4709/3100	$5027/3200
1970[2]	$4500/3000	$4800/3100	$4800/3100	$5100/3200

1 GT-500KR approx. 100 lbs heavier; prices: fastback $4473, convertible $4594
2 weights and prices estimated

Engine Availability

Type	cid	bhp	1965	1966	1967 GT-350	1967 GT-500	1968 GT-350	1968 GT-500	1969-70 GT-350	1969-70 GT-500
ohv V-8	289	306	●	●						
ohv V-8	289	290[1]			●					
ohv V-8	302	250					●			
ohv V-8	302	350[1,2]					●			
ohv V-8	351	290							●	
ohv V-8	390	335						●		
ohv V-8	427	390				●				
ohv V-8	428	360						●		
ohv V-8	428	375[1]								●
ohv V-8	428	400[1]				●		●[3]		

1 estimated; advertised bhp different
2 supercharged
3 GT-500KR

And happily, the last Shelby-Mustangs wouldn't be the last Shelbys. Being who he is, Carroll couldn't stay away from the car business forever. Today, thanks to his friend Iacocca, he's working the same kind of magic at Chrysler that he did for Ford, and we enthusiasts are all the better for it.

One interesting postscript: In 1981, exactly 15 years after Shelby had ordered up those six prototype GT-350 convertibles, another 12 were converted from restored '66 Mustang ragtops with his blessing—essentially brand-new cars identical with the originals. All sold quickly despite costing $40,000 apiece. Then again, what price history—or a sure-fire investment?

The '69 GT-500 fastback (*opposite*) retailed for $4709; a total of 1536 were built. The 1970 Shelbys, about 600 of them, were reserialed '69s that received two black stripes on the hood and a Boss 302-type spoiler on the front valence for differentiation. After these were sold, the Shelby Mustang became history.

INDEX

A

Allegro X-car, 50, 51
Anaheim development program, 174
Arizona development program, 171
Ash, L. David, 51, 174, 176
Auto 1987, 272
Automotive News, 223
Avventura, 50

B

Bailey, J. Edward, 58
Bidwell, Ben, 173
Bordinat, Eugene, 46, 47, 51, 58, 160,
    170, 172, 174
Boyer, Bill, 25
Breech, Ernest R., 23, 221
Brock, Pete, 295
Brooker, Brad, 290
Bucknum, Ronnie, 298
Buick
    Skylark, 19, 20
    Riviera, 28

C

Cadillac
    Eldorado, 20
Caldwell, Philip, 232
Cantwell, Chuck, 284
Capri, 15, 16
Car and Driver, 49, 133, 237, 238,
    296, 305
Car Life, 133
Cardinal project, 49
Case, Tom, 23, 25
Chevrolet
    Corvair, 29, 31
    Corvette, 22, 23
Cobra 289, 282
Cobra 427, 282
Cole, Ed, 22, 36
Conley, John, 54
CONSUMER GUIDE® magazine, 237
Continental
    Mark II, 25
    Mark III, 25
Cougar II, 51, 52
Crusoe, Lewis D., 25

D

DeLaRossa, Don, 172, 174, 200
Detroit *Free Press*, 58
Dinkel, John, 220
Donner, Matt, 124
Donohue, Mark, 106, 290, 298, 300
Dowd, Ken, 114
Dragonsnake, 292

E

Earl, Harley, 22, 36
Esquire, 58

F

Feaheny, Tom, 91, 92, 124
Fairlane Group, 42, 50
Fearsome Fords, 121
Federation Internationale de l'Automobile
    (FIA), 47
Follmer, George, 298, 310
Ford
    Custom Crestliner, 15, 16
    Futura, 32
    Probe, 268
    Sportsman, 14
    Sprint, 32
    Thunderbird, 23, 25, 27
    Victoria, 16
    See also Mustang.
Ford, Henry, 25, 113
Ford II, Henry, 14, 23, 25, 39, 42, 51,
    52, 54, 58, 113, 144, 221, 232
Ford II, Walter Buhl, 58
Frey, Donald N., 43, 51

G

Gerstenberger, Todd, 228
Glonka, Ray, 58
Gregorie, Bob, 14
Gurney, Dan, 49, 82, 298, 312

H

Haas, Gary, 210
Halderman, Gail, 52, 117

Hall, Ed, 114
Hall, Jim, 312
Hall, Phil, 121
Hampson, R.J., 144
Hane, Walter, 290
Harper, Peter, 82
Hershey, Frank, 25
Hot Rod, 106
Hudson Italia, 22
Humphries, Ross, 90

I

Iacocca, Lee, 33, 36, 38, 39, 40, 42, 43,
    49, 51, 52, 54, 58, 81, 87, 108,
    144, 145, 160, 168, 170, 171, 172,
    173, 174, 220, 221, 222, 223, 232,
    262, 312, 315
Indianapolis 500 *1979*, 225
Irvin, Robert W., 144

J

Johnson, Robert, 290
Jones, Parnelli, 298, 310

K

Kaiser
    Dragon, 16
    Virginian, 16
Kaiser-Darrin, 22
Kaiser-Frazer
    Jade Dragon, 17
    Mark II Dragon, 17
Knudsen, Semon E. "Bunkie," 112, 113,
    114, 124, 128, 141, 144, 145,
    146, 221
Knudsen, William S., 113, 221
Koch, Chuck, 153
Kopka, Don, 274
Kranefuss, Michael, 228
Kwech, Horst, 310

L

Labor Day Nationals *1965*, 82
Lawton, Bill, 82

Le Mans 24 Hours *1959*, 282
Life, 58
Lincoln Lido, 15
Loewy, Raymond, 22
Look, 58
Ludwig, Klaus, 228
Lunn, Roy, 46, 47

M
Maguire, Robert, 25
Mayhew, Fritz, 210
Mazda Mustang, 268
McHose, Chuck, 295
McNamara, Robert S., 25, 27, 33, 36,
    38, 39, 40

Mecham, Dennis, 228
Median, 50
Mercury
    Monterey, 15, 16
    Sportsman, 14
Miles, Ken, 284
Mina, 50

Misch, Herb, 44
Mitchell, William L., 28, 36, 91, 114
Moore, Bud, 298, 310, 312
Morsey Jr., Chase, 43
Motor Trend, 81, 87, 136, 153
Mountain, Chuck, 114
Mueller, Al, 173

Mustang
  Boss 302, 112, 113, 124, 126, 128,
    133, 136, 141, 149, 301, 306, 310,
    311, 312
  Boss 351, 149, 153, 158, 159
  Boss 429, 128, 130, 133, 136, 306
  California Special, 108, 300

Cobra Jet, 113, 122, 124, 136, 150
Cobra II, 184, 188
427, 102, 104, 105
Grandé, 112, 120, 133, 138
Ghia, 180, 181, 184, 192, 226
GT, 84, 101, 234, 236, 239, 240, 255,
  257, 258, 262, 270, 272, 274

King Cobra, 188, 192
LX, 270, 274, 276
LX 5.0 Sport, 276
Mach 1, 112, 113, 120, 121, 122, 124,
    133, 136, 138, 141, 148, 150, 151,
    159, 162, 180, 184, 301, 306
Mach 2, 114

I, 44, 46, 47, 49
Stallion, 184
Super Cobra Jet, 150
SVO, 249, 251, 252, 253, 257, 258,
    259, 270
Turbo GT, 244-45, 247, 254
II, 51, 168, 170, 172, 174, 178, 179,

    180, 184, 187, 188, 192, 195, 198,
    204, 205, 216, 218, 232
2+2, 68
390, 96, 104
1965-1966, 56-87
1967-1968, 88-109
1969-1970, 110-41

1971-1973, 142-65
1974-1978, 166-95
1979-1981, 196-229
1982-1986, 230-59
1987, 270, 274
1988, 276
1989, 276, 279
See also Mazda Mustang; Shelby-
    Mustang.

N
Nance, James J., 19, 46
Nash-Healey, 22
National Hot Rod Association, 292
Naughton, John, 133, 136
New York World's Fair *1964*, 58
Newsweek, 36, 39, 58

O
Ohio development program, 171, 172
Oldsmobile Fiesta, 19
Olmsted, Fred, 58
Oros, Joe, 51, 52, 58, 173

P
Packard Caribbean, 18, 19
Passino, Jacque, 122
Pearson, David, 298
Penske, Roger, 298, 300, 312
Petersen, Donald, 232, 233, 262
Petit, Dick, 114
Petrany, Zoltan, 290
Popular Science, 82

Posey, Sam, 311, 312
Prendergast, Jack J., 52
Proctor, Peter, 82

R
Rees, David, 210
Revson, Peter, 298, 310
Gas Rhonda, 82
Ritchey, Les, 82
Road & Track, 51, 52, 66, 76, 80, 81,
    82, 181, 184, 220, 296
Roush, Jack, 277

S
Shannon, Bill, 114
Shelby, Carroll, 52, 98, 256, 282, 292, 293
    296, 298, 301, 306, 311, 314, 315
Shelby GT, 285, 287
Shelby-Mustang, 281-315
    GT-350, 256, 282, 287, 290, 291, 292,
        293, 295, 298, 299, 305, 306
    GT-500, 296, 299, 305, 306
    GT-500KR, 299
    R-model, 287, 290
    S-model, 285, 287, 290
Sherman, Don, 237, 238
Shinoda, Larry, 114, 124, 146
Sperlich, Hal, 92, 173
Sports Car Club of America (SCCA),
    47, 106, 124, 282, 283, 285, 289,
    295, 300, 312
Sports Car Graphic, 295
Stevens, Brooks, 28
Stevenson, R.L., 144

Stroppe, Bill, 292
Studebaker Gran Turismo Hawk, 28, 29

T
Telnack, Jack, 174, 205, 208, 210, 2
Time, 36, 40, 58
Titus, Jerry, 290, 295, 298, 300, 3
Tour de France *1963*, 82
Trans-American Sedan Champion
    1966, 124
    1970, 312
    1971, 312

U
United States Grand Prix
    1962, 49
    1963, 51
U.S. News & World Report, 58

V
Van Buren, Fred, 290

W
Wall Street Journal, 58
Winn, Harvey, 114
Witzenburg, Gary, 90, 117
Woods, Damon, 25
Woods, Michael, 214
Wykes, Harry, 228

Y
Yates, Brock, 305, 306